THE TALE-TELLER

THE TALE-TELLERS

A Short Study of Humankind

NANCY HUSTON

McArthur & Company
Toronto

English edition first published in Canada in 2008 by
McArthur & Company
322 King St. West, Suite 402
Toronto, ON
M5V 1J2
www.mcarthur-co.com

First published in French by Actes Sud Leméac, 2008

Library and Archives Canada Cataloguing in Publication

Huston, Nancy, 1953-
[Espèce fabulatrice. English]
The tale-tellers : a short study of humankind / Nancy Huston.

Translation of: L'espèce fabulatrice.
ISBN 978-1-55278-754-0

I. Title. II. Title: Espèce fabulatrice. English.

PS8565.U8255Z46513 2008   C848'.5403   C2008-905166-1

Cover Art: James Abbott McNeill Whistler, Nocturne in Black and Gold,
the Falling Rocket (detail), 1875, The Bridgeman Art Library
Printed in Canada by Webcom

The publisher would like to acknowledge the financial support of the
Government of Canada through the Book Publishing Industry Development
Program (BPIDP) and the Canada Council for our publishing activities.
The publisher further wishes to acknowledge the financial support
of the Ontario Arts Council for our publishing program.

10 9 8 7 6 5 4 3 2 1

To my father

"Nothing is human that does not aspire to the imaginary."
– Romain Gary

Table of Contents

THE QUESTION

Suddenly the prisoner who had been stubbornly silent up until now raised her head, stared me straight in the face, and asked, "What's the point of making up stories when reality is already so incredible?"

The woman was prostrate. She had killed somebody; I had not. My murders were all in my novels.

We were in the women's prison at Fleury-Mérogis, some twenty miles outside of Paris. The other members of the reading club glanced at me expectantly, waiting to see what sort of an answer I would come up with. The silence lengthened, and I felt an abyss opening up between these women and myself, for there was no denying that their reality was more incredible than mine. Plausible scenes from their incredible reality started flashing through my mind – scenes rife with blood, knives, guns, bombs, screams, drugs, blows, disorder, poverty, anguish, sleepless nights, bad dreams, alcoholism, rape, despair and confusion ...

What could I say? "To give shape to reality"? No, I could not say that. It would have been insufficient – absurdly, woundingly insufficient – and also pretentious, somehow. It couldn't possibly be the right answer, whereas this woman was desperate for an answer.

I began to rack my brains ...

I

THE BIRTH OF MEANING

*"People always think seagulls' cries are filled with
angst, whereas in fact they do not mean a thing; it's
our own psychology that has this effect on us.
Everywhere we go we see stuff that does not exist; it's
all going on inside of us, we are like ventriloquists
that make everything talk – seagulls, the sky,
the wind, everything ..."*
– Romain Gary

Animals, the lot of us.

Mammals, super-superior primates, et cetera. With no
more reason to be on planet Earth, or do anything here,
than any other species, on this planet or any other.

Yet we are special.

All animals, diversely, record reality and respond to it. Their senses transmit incomplete information to their brains, which use this information to build up the image of a complete world. They draw conclusions to the best of their abilities, communicate these conclusions to one another, cooperate, do what they can to survive.

Our specialty, our prerogative, our mania, our glory and our downfall, is the question why.

But why the why? Where does it come from?
It comes from time.
And where does time come from?

From the fact that we alone, of all animal species, know how we were born, and that we will die.

Our awareness of these two phenomena gives us what even our closest relatives (chimps and bonobos) do not have – namely, the notion of what a *lifetime is*.

We alone see our existence on Earth as a *path* endowed with meaning (and direction). An arc. A curve that takes us from birth to death. A shape that unfolds in time, with a beginning, a series of adventures, and an end. In other words: *a narrative*.

"In the beginning was the Word" means only this – that the Word (action endowed with meaning) marks the beginning of our species.

Narrative gives our life a dimension of meaning utterly unknown to animals. Thus, from now on, I shall give it a capital letter. Human Meaning is distinct from animal meaning in that it is built up out of narratives, stories, fictions.

* * *

The universe as such has no Meaning. It is silent.

No one put Meaning into the world – no one but us.

Meaning depends on humanity, and humanity depends on Meaning.

When we become extinct, even if our sun continues to emit heat and light, there will be no Meaning left anywhere. No tears will be shed over our disappearance; no conclusions drawn as to what our passage through the universe signified; its signification will end with us.

Like Nature, humans abhor a vaccum. We are literally incapable of recording reality without instantly "understanding" it. And we understand it essentially through narratives, that is, fictions.

Unlike other animals, we are not content to record, build up, deduce the meaning of the events going on around us. No, we require that this meaning *unfold* – and what allows it to unfold is not language but narrative. This is why all human groups have developed means for *measuring and marking* time (rituals, dates, calendars, seasonal festivals, and so forth); these are indispensable to narrative.

Monkeys can learn thousands of words; they can convey meaning through the use of linguistic symbols, but they cannot tell stories.

They cannot even say to each other: "Meet you here tomorrow, same time, same place!"

When a herd of antilope reaches a riverbed and finds it has gone dry, they either look for water elsewhere or die of thirst. Humans, faced with the same disturbing observation, even as they look for water elsewhere, and before they die of thirst, *interpret*. They pray, dance, look for guilty parties, undertake propitiatory rituals to convince the spirits to send rain ...

In a word, they elevate meaning into Meaning.

We translate, metaphorize, metamorphose – *everything*. Yes, even in the post-Enlightenment, disenchanted, scientific, rational Western world.

For life is "nasty, brutish and short," and our species is the only one to know it.

* * *

For us humans, ever since we started living in time, there is no such thing as real-reality; always and only fictional-reality.

Narrativity evolved in our species as a survival technique. It is inscribed in the very circumvolutions of our brains. Weaker than the other species, over millions of years of evolution, *Homo sapiens* learned to reap the benefits of endowing reality with meaning through tale-telling.

All of us do it – involuntarily, unwittingly, unceasingly.

The life of primates on planet Earth is filled with threats and dangers. All higher primates strive to protect themselves by sending signals to one another; only we humans chatter, blather, make up stories to survive – and then, also to survive, believe most adamantly in our inventions.

Speech never contents itself with naming or describing reality. Always and everywhere, it *narrates* (i.e., *invents*) reality.

Reality is nameless. There is no such thing as the "accurate" or "natural" name of anything, whether object, action, or feeling.

As far back as you can climb in etymologies, all you ever find as you swing from word to word are other words, that is, other arbitrary signs, cutting up the universe, constructing their objects rather than finding them.

We are the ones who engendered them. They are real, since they are part of our reality, but they are not "true."

Without human beings – no names.

God naming the first humans, etc., is a fiction. We are not God's creation, He is ours.

God cannot *be*, except in our stories. In order to *be*, He would need to speak; in order to speak He would need a language, and to have a language He would need to be part of human history.

God and the gods are indeed a part of this history, only they systematically refuse to admit it.

Your name, as well, is a fiction. It could be other than what it is. You can change it. Women do so all the time. In marrying, they switch from one fiction to another.

Baptism, marriage: acts of magic.

All nomination is magical.

Human beings are unwitting magicians.

Money is a fiction – little scraps of paper that have been decreed to represent gold. Gold is a fiction – worth no more, in the absolute, than sand. The Stock Exchange is one gigantic fiction.

Human beings are unwitting alchemists – through the tales they tell, they turn everything into money, that is, gold.

Our inventions are not *lies*, since we adhere to them in all good faith. It is in our interest to adhere to them.

If language were content to reflect reality, why would every tongue invent words that should not be pronounced?

Swearwords are one of the great proofs of humanity.

Computers and chimpanzees can neither lie, write poetry, nor hurl insults at each other – three ordinary forms of human magic which entail the deliberate use of one word to mean another.

Stories (in particular, written stories) build bridges between past and present, present and future; they enable both past and future to exist in the present.

The other higher primates live in the present. A chimp can extrapolate from the past to make better decisions in the present, but it can project itself neither into the past (especially before its own birth!) nor into the future (especially after its own death!)

Thus, chimps do not lie awake at night worrying about death; nor are they filled with hope, nostalgia, and so forth. ... All these affects hinge on narrativity – that is, the specifically human mania for endowing reality with Meaning.

Meaning is our hard drug. In the form of political or religious ideals, it is not only hard but pure. To get a dose of it, people are willing to sacrifice the lives of their loved ones ... and even their own lives (*cf.* human bombers).

* * *

The other higher primates value the group to which they belong and are prepared to fight ferociously to defend it against other groups. They know how to console, attack, help, and betray each other. ... In a word, they feel *empathy*; they can see the world through eyes other than their own and are thus capable, like ourselves, of both cruelty and compassion. What characterizes human beings is not that they behave kindly or nastily, cruelly or compassionately, but that they tell themselves they are behaving this way *for* something. And that "something" (whether a religion, a nation, or a family line) is invariably a fiction.

* * *

What does man's entry into time and Meaning give him? Something no monkey has: a *self*.

I is a fiction.

The surprising truth is that it is easier to see the world through another's eyes than through one's own. We do not need narrativity to put ourselves in someone else's shoes, but we need it to put ourselves in our own. The difference between monkeys and humans is exactly the difference between intelligence and consciousness – between the *fact* of existing and the *sense* of existing. Between "want to do that" and "why am I here?".

Consciousness is *intelligence plus time* – that is, narrativity.

We absorb it along with our mother tongue. It is not: first I learn individual words, and then I learn to string them together into a story. Rather, it is: *I* – a whole story, in and of itself!

The human and the chimpanzee foetus are similarly curled up in their mother's wombs, similarly delivered, washed, fed, and cared for by their mothers. Chimpanzee parents do not, however, name their babies, sing lullabies to them, or teach them about their genealogy.

The human child will learn to say *I*; the chimp child will not.

As they enter our brains, fictions shape and transform them. It is less we who create them than they who create us – modelling for each of us, over the course of our early childhood, a *self*.

Selves are made, not born. The *I* is the result of a lengthy and laborious construction. Far from being always-already there, waiting to affirm itself, it is first an empty frame, then a mobile configuration, which we think of as fixed only through convention.

To dispose of a self, you have to learn to fabulate. Though we conveniently tend to forget this afterwards, it took us a lot of time, and a lot of help from others, to become somebody. It took layers and layers of impressions connected into stories. Songs. Fairy-tales. Exclamations. Gestures. Rules. Socialization. Clean. Dirty. Say this. Do not do that. Bing, bang, bong.

That is humanization. Only afterwards, and only very gradually, can the *I* emerge. Its memories will also be organized into stories.

The *I*: a chromosomic dice-toss strung with fictions.

Thus, even with cloning, no two *I*'s could ever be identical, for no two series of fictions can be identical.

To become (or rather to *create*) a self is to activate the narrative mechanism within a particular familial and cultural context, one that is unique by definition.

* * *

People who think it "strange" (or "unfortunate," or "incredible," or "unfair") that we cannot recall the events of early childhood do not know what it is to be human.

We have no memories of our early childhood because there was not yet an *I* on which to string fictions. Our way of recording reality back then was so different from what it is now that it has become illegible to us. All we can do is guess at it through the fugitive traces it left – in our dreams, our artworks, our mental illnesses.

Our memory is a construction, a fiction. This does not imply that it is false. Rather, it implies that with no conscious intervention on our part, it is perpetually involved in associating, articulating, selecting, excluding, and forgetting – that is, constructing; that is, confabulating.

We say, "Tell me the story of your life," because there is no way we could possibly tell each other *our lives* (even *after* the age of six, when the *I* with its specific memories has firmly settled into place).

Tolstoy in his youth once set about writing *The Story of Yesterday*. He gave up the attempt after a couple of hundred pages, having come to see that he had set himself an impossible task.

I swear to tell the whole truth? We can say true things, but never the whole truth – not even about what has happened in the room we are in over the past five minutes. We cannot tell it because it is infinite. In order to preserve our *selves*, we need to leave out almost everything.

Every tiny detail of your experience between birth and death would require an infinite amount of time to be exhaustively explained. Thus, to give me an idea of who you are – to "tell me the story of your life" – not only do you need to forget millions of things, you need to omit other millions. Of necessity, you will select the events you deem the most salient, relevant, or important, and organize them into narratives.

In other words, very innocently, you will spin tales. Using the same techniques as professional novelists, all of us create the novels of our lives.

Childhood narratives (like dream narratives) give psychoanalysts a choice terrain for studying their patients' *style*, their preferred fictional ploys. Few or no verifiable facts; no reality check – a heyday for interpretation!

Freud listened, goggle-eyed, to his patients' family romances. His great discovery: *what matters is what is Meaningful to the patient, and only that.*

All of us spin tales about our stay on Earth. Or to put it more accurately, we are these tales. "I" is the way in which I perceive and narrate the sum total of my experiences.

Consciousness is neither more nor less than the pronounced penchant of our brain for all things stable, continuous, reasonable, and relatable.

When our fictionalizing *I* dissolves – when it grows incapable of effectively (and imperceptibly) constructing, organizing, inventing, excluding, interpreting, explaining what is going on around it – "reality" becomes illegible to us.

In the final stages of Alzheimer's disease, for instance, we can still talk, but we can no longer interpret. We are still alive, but the story of our lives is over.

* * *

Where is human reality? In the fictions that make it up.

No one is responsible for these fictions. They are not the result of a plot of the powerful against the powerless. No one decided to invent them. Fictions permeate the human world. To say that a world is human is to say that it is permeated with fictions.

When I say fictions, I do not mean silly games. I do not mean – as the heavyset mover put it, puffing and sweating as he lugged my dozens of boxes of books from one apartment to another – "Bubbles! Nothing but bubbles!"

When I say fictions, I mean human (that is, constructed) realities.

My life, like everyone else's, depends on them.

The Huns, the Mongols, the Nazis, the members of the N.K.V.D., barbarians of yesterday and today, from the North and from the South, were all firmly convinced that they were living in reality – whereas their minds, like everyone else's, were teeming with fantasies, myths, and legends designed to rationalize, justify, and glorify their depredations and massacres, their plunderings and blood-baths.

People who think they are living in reality are ignorant, and their ignorance is potentially murderous.

To us human beings, fictions are as real as the ground beneath our feet; indeed they *are* that ground, our support and sustenance in the world.

No one has ever come across a human population that was content to live in reality – i.e., without religion, taboo, ritual, genealogy, fairy-tales, magic, stories – i.e., without recourse to the imagination, without confabulation.

Because of the faith we place in them, the fictions we have concocted over the centuries are our most precious and incontrovertible reality. Shot through and through with imagination, they give rise to *a second level of reality* – human reality, universal despite its widely varying appearances over space and time.

Rooted in these fictions, *made up* of them, human consciousness is a fabulous machine – and an *innately tale-telling one*.

We are the tale-telling species.

II

I, FICTION

"The truth? What truth? Perhaps the truth is
that I do not exist."
— Romain Gary

We weave our identities. Their warp and woof are the tales, histories, countless fictions inculcated into us in early childhood. We adhere to these fictions, feel strongly about them, cling to them – whereas, of course, had we been adopted as babies on the opposite side of the globe, taught that we were Australian not Canadian, Protestant not Jewish, Conservative not Liberal, and so forth, we would have turned into someone very different.

A case in point: Romain Gary's novel *The Life Before Us*. A number of prostitutes' children in the lower-class Parisian neighbourhood of Belleville are being cared for by

Madame Rosa, an ageing Jewess who used to be a prostitute herself. Her favourite child is "Momo" – Mohamed, now fourteen, who has no memory of his parents. Knowing him to be of Muslim stock, Madame Rosa has always encouraged him to hang out with Mr. Hamed, an elderly rug salesman from Algeria who teaches him verses from the Koran and occasionally takes him to the mosque. One day, Momo's father suddenly turns up: he is ill, he says, and wants to take his son back. Madame Rosa is indignant, for not only did this man murder his wife (Momo's mother), but also he never sent a single cheque for his son's upkeep. Madame Rosa, who is determined not to lose Momo, comes up with a brilliant idea – she calls him "Moses," and gaily assures his father that he has been raised as a good Jew. He only eats kosher food, he has had his bar mitzvah, and so forth. The father's eyes pop out of his head. "I gave you an Arab son in good condition and I want an Arab son in return. I absolutely do not want a Jewish son!" he shouts. "Oh dear, oh dear," says Madame Rosa (who knows all about the fictional nature of identity), "I must have raised Mohamed as Moses and Moses as Mohamed. I received them both on the same day and I guess I got them mixed up." Horrified, the father has a conniption fit and dies on the spot.

* * *

Nomination: magic.

Language orders our experience, making it possible for us to communicate. As long as our definitions coincide, we understand each other and it works.

Language confers order. We tend to forget, however, that *order* is not synonymous with *truth*.

For human beings, no truths are given.

All truths are constructed – through fictions.

* * *

Let's say that in view of making out an ID card for me, you ask me to fill out a form.

You warn me in advance that my answers must be free of any and all fiction, because you want to know who I "really" am.

All right, I'll take a shot at it. What do I know for sure about my identity? What can I tell you about myself that involves only pure, undiluted reality?

My given name?
That is the first fiction.

Our parents (the *authors* of our days) hesitate, sometimes up to the last minute, as to the names they want to give their children, just as novelists do for the names of their characters.

Once a name is given, it becomes a reality. There is no contradiction between reality and fiction. Fiction is human reality.

Recording the name in the town hall register is like publishing a book – from then on, the die is cast; there is no going back. On September 15th, 1953, my name could still have been Alice. As of September 16th, it truly was Nancy.

Being only a few hours old, I did not know it yet (not yet having a self with which to know it), but these sounds would gradually be imprinted on my brain (or, to put it more lyrically, they would "crystallize in my mind") and contribute to the creation of that self.

No one *has* a name.

All of us *receive* one that has been pumped full of

Meaning. Before landing on us, it belonged to a saint, an ancestor, the dedicatee of a famous song, the character of a novel, opera, or television series ...

By definition, it comes down to us from another place, time, person. We enter life through a connection with the past.

Parents are not allowed to make up names for their children out of the blue.

My parents could not have called me *Bzyingak*.

The given name is an excellent example of how the arbitrary becomes necessary, how fiction shapes reality. Though our given names could obviously have been other than what they are, they *are* what they are, and we cannot claim that they leave us indifferent. Every word that has the same initial as our first name, or rhymes with it, will be powerfully marked in our brains. (I jump every time someone yells "Taxi!" in the street.)

So be it: "I" shall be called *Nancy*, my maternal grandmother's nickname, and *Louise*, my paternal grandmother's middle name. Both of these women received their names from someone else, who received them from someone else in turn, and so on. We are magically connected to one another through these tiny flashes of fictive Meaning, leaping backwards through the years, decades, or centuries.

No more than Rome, the *I* is not built in a day.

Though now endowed with a given name, I still need to learn huge numbers of things before I can utter the word *I* and know what I mean by it.

For instance: where my mother's body ends and my own begins.

And also – crucially – sphincter control (how to restrain my impulse to pee and poo whenever and wherever I feel like it).

Chimpanzee mothers do not tell their little ones: "Wipe yourself carefully and do not forget to flush the toilet." Or: "Look, you wet your bed again – no dessert tonight."

There can be no knowing without *no*-ing – i.e., without taboos.

Taboos, too, are fictions – ones that help to structure life in society. They vary enormously from one society to another; what matters is that *they* exist.

My family name?
Soon I shall master this as well – the name that I have inherited from my father, and that connects me to the other members of my family.

My mother's family name, exactly as valid (or invalid) as my father's, will be consigned to oblivion.

This is how our civilization has been doing things, these past few centuries. Other civilizations do them differently, using various combinations of patronyms and matronyms. Whichever system gets chosen, it is merely a convention, a convenience.

Just imagine if we had to recite the names of *all* our ancestors – introductions would be interminable! Our names would be legion, like the devil's. We need to simplify. Thus, in our part of the world, people generally have two names, one given, one family (in Russia: three).

Here again, what matters is that *a choice be made.* Whatever the content of that choice, it will be ratified as a necessity. So be it: my name is Huston. As good a name as any other, inherited from my father's paternal Irish strain. Its spelling is moot (Houston, Hueston, etc.) – as is often the case in preponderantly illiterate populations. Probable etymology: "Hugh's Town."

But who the hell was Hugh? *"What's Montague?"* says Juliet when she falls in love with Romeo. *"It is nor hand, nor foot, / Nor arm, nor face, nor any other part / Belonging to a man."* What is this hypothetical Hugh of yesteryear to me that I should have to bear his name my whole life long? Of course, I could choose to bear my husband's name instead, in which case I would be known – O supreme fiction – as Mrs. Todorov, that is, Gift-of-God.

No worries. The main thing, where names are concerned, is to have one – and, through it, to feel connected to one's progenitors. Which is the case, here as everywhere. Whew.

Had I been abandoned at birth then adopted by another family, I would have inherited *that* family's patronym. Simpson, for instance. *Simpson* would have been part of my identity, as firmly as *Huston* is today. Who knows? It might even have been decked out with a particle – *Madame de Simpson*, and I could have taken pride in *that*. To say nothing of a title – *Madame the Marquess of Simpson!*

The name Huston constrains me, among other things, not to copulate with other Hustons of my entourage, my close male relatives.

The Elementary Structures of Kinship: thus begins the circulation of women, words, and stories, strengthening the bonds among human groups.

None of us has a "real" name – one that is "truly" us.

All of us inhabit our names – or rather, *learn* to inhabit them.

My name really is Nancy Huston. That's the way things are ... but they could have been otherwise.

"Names – pseudonyms, the lot of them." (Romain Gary)

My date of birth?
Only human beings measure time.

In the eternity of the universe, there are no dates.

My birthdate depends on a whole other series of human conventions.

Because of the domination of the Roman Church some fifteen hundred years ago, it was decreed that the birth of a certain Jesus would be called Year One.

It so happens I came out of my mother's tummy one thousand nine hundred and fifty-three years after Jesus came out of *his*.

According to the Hebraic calendar, however, I was born in a different year; according to the Muslim calendar in another still, and so forth.

Perhaps if I manage to save humanity, the day will come when people will say that Jesus was born in 1953 before N.H.?

My place of birth?
I can recite, as children love to do, the boxes-within-boxes, declaring proudly: I was born in the city of Calgary in the province of Alberta in the country of Canada in the continent of North America on planet Earth in the galaxy of the Milky Way ...

The problem is that all these names, too, are figures of speech (*Calgary* means clear running water, the *Milky Way* is neither milky nor a way, and so forth) – they, too, have a history.

Not a particularly long one, as it happens. A mere century before my birth, "Calgary" and "Alberta" did not exist, the Forty-Ninth Parallel that stakes out Canada's southern border had not yet been traced, and all of those places bore different names, given them by the Indian tribes then living there (though of course it's also a fiction to call them Indian, Christopher Columbus having believed he had landed in India).

You say your own country, city, and continent are "older" than mine? All right, but so what? Does that by any chance make you superior to me? Their names are every bit as fictitious as Canadian place names; they, too, came into being at a specific moment in History.

From eternity's point of view, there is no difference at all between 2000 BC and 2000 CE.

For whatever reason, the Blackfoot, Cree, Gros Ventre, and other Indian tribes are not currently contesting our decision to call the region of my birth "Alberta" (in honour of some British princess or other). That does not make Alberta a natural or an historical name.

Manifest destiny / divine right / the representatives of the Queen of England (multiple choice) decided that the white man could force the natives onto reserves and settle this whole territory and give it another name.

In other parts of the world – the Middle East, for instance – people kill each other every day for that sort of decision.

"My ancestors lived here fifty years ago."
"Yes, but mine lived here two thousand years ago."
"Abraham's zoning ordinance gives us the right to live here."
"Our God decreed that this land belonged to us."

Chimpanzees have a different take on things. True, they inhabit territories and are prepared to fight if necessary to defend them– but they do not live in countries.

To invest place names with Meaning, you need to know the stories to which they refer, understand the connections they imply and impose. Then you need to accept those fictions as true and valid.

When you think about it, human babies do not live in countries, either. At the age of six months, I lived in neither Calgary nor Canada. Only very gradually did I come to grasp and conceptualize the concentric circles of which my thinking brain was the centre: my body, my crib, my bedroom, at the very most my house ... but I was oblivious to the rest of the world.

When they reach the age of five or six, human children are also taught to identify with (and be proud of) their neighbourhoods, villages, cities, countries. In my case, the acquisition of this pride was made problematic by the fact that my family moved house constantly, zigzagging around the continent from Alberta to Texas to Ontario, then back to Alberta, finally winding up in New Hampshire, two thousand miles east of my "hometown." What could I be proud of when, finding myself in a different school every two or three years, I would have to pass muster as "the new pupil"? It was not always easy. ... Looking back on it, though, I realize that having to constantly switch "points of view," put myself in other people's shoes and see the world through their eyes in addition to my own, turned out to be excellent practice for my future vocation as a novelist.

What else can I be sure of, identity-wise?

My genealogy?
That I am the daughter of This Woman and That Man?

Indisputably, I am the chromosomic cross of those two individuals. That, however, is not really – or not *essentially* – what makes them my parents. Here again, with the same genetic imprint, the same DNA structure, I would harbour completely different convictions about my identity had I been adopted by a couple of Trobrianders. No, those two people are my parents *essentially* because they were the first people who talked to me. Thanks to them, I absorbed and digested a certain number of *stories* about my relatives and ancestors – stories that penetrated to the depths of my consciousness, and contributed to making me who I am.

My sex?
Ha, ha, very funny. I'm a female, no doubt about it. Frankly, though, that's nothing to make a fuss about. For better and for worse, the specialty – no, the specificity – of human beings is making a fuss about everything.

My religion?
Religions are one of the primary sources of the fables that bond people together.

My father being of Methodist and my mother of Presbyterian stock, they opted upon marrying for a *third* variety of Protestantism, and thus had their three children baptized into the Unitarian Church. After they divorced, my father married a Catholic woman from Germany; the two of them in turn reached a compromise and we children were therefore rebaptized – this time into the Anglican Church. A few years after my Confirmation, I took a philosophy course and stopped believing in God;

my father later converted to Buddhism; each of my siblings embarked on a different spiritual path ...

In other words, I had the good fortune of learning at an early age about the fictional nature of religious appurtenance.

My racial or ethnic makeup?
Come on. I'm a mixture, just like everybody else. My ancestors came to Canada from all sorts of European countries, including ones that "hated" each other (Ireland and Scotland, England and Germany). Upon arriving in the New World, the males probably fooled around with some Indian females. ... Despite their desperate attempts to keep things straight in this area, human beings tend to copulate left and right, making babies both in and out of wedlock. Pure blood is one of humanity's most persistent and pernicious fictions.

My skin is what is generally though inaccurately termed "white." Thus, whether I like it or not, my history is inextricably linked to that of "Whites" all over the world. I am made acutely and unpleasantly aware of this every time I go for a stroll in Harlem (USA), Diamant (Martinique), or Johannesburg (South Africa).

My language?
My great-grandparents' German and Gaelic having been

eliminated from the picture, melting-pot *oblige*, the only language I learned in early childhood was English, specifically the mid-twentieth-century Canadian variant of that language, the result of countless compromises and readjustments among other variants (British, American Scots, aristocratic, cockney) – each of which had itself been shaped over the centuries by Latin, Greek, Saxon, Celtic, and so forth.

Arbitrary though it was, this language left its indelible imprint on me. More than that: it *made* me – setting up the circuits of synapses in the left hemisphere of my brain that would eventually bring forth the ideas, opinions, perceptions, and judgments I think of as my "self."

At the age of six, I spent a few months in Germany and learned to speak German; then, throughout my years of schooling in Canada, I was taught French as well – because, due to unresolved colonial rivalry between France and Great Britain in the eighteenth century, my country happens to be partly francophone.

Instead of being concentrated in the left hemisphere like my mother tongue, my acquired languages (French, German, scraps of Italian, Spanish, and Portuguese) would be "bilateralized" – that is, distributed over various regions in both brain hemispheres. Having been acquired after my toilet-training, these languages would be connected to no interiorized taboos. Thus, I would find their swearwords merely quaint; they would not "get to me" the way English swearwords do.

Speaking one or more foreign languages effectively destroys the specious self-evidence of the mother tongue, helping us see it for what it is – namely, *one of any number of possible "takes" on reality.*

My professional activity?
To be is to do, as Sartre said. In other words, one becomes a writer by writing.

What happens if I fall ill and can no longer write? What happens if I retire? What happens to actors who can't find work, or to assembly-line workers who get laid off? The Marxist dogma according to which people derive their identities from their economic activities opens up vast new possibilities for coherent fictional existence – and also, when those activities collapse, vast new possibilities for madness.

As a rule, professions whose roles are rigid and whose "lines" are fixed in advance also have fixed costumes to go with them. Such is the case for soldiers, popes, bishops, judges, prostitutes, and so forth (cf. Genet's *The Balcony*).

Writers, who make up their own lines as they go along, have no particular costume.

My diplomas, prizes, medals?
Yes, yes, of course. Very cute, very clinky. So many accessories I can pin onto the character I think of as my self, so that it can puff up its chest when it walks out onto the stage of the world.

My political affiliation?
Now, let's see. I can proclaim it by putting a French, a Canadian, or a French-Canadian flag in my window ... by gluing a fist-clutching-rose sticker onto my bumper ... by wearing a Palestinian *keffiyeh*, a red scarf, a Lorraine Cross, a T-shirt embossed with the portrait of Jean-Marie Le Pen. All of these things can reassure me, and inform you, as to my identity in this area.

More useful and effective fictions which, like religions, give shape and Meaning to our lives.

There you have it – I cannot say a single word about myself without dragging along the infinite baggage of world history.

I have finished filling out my ID form, and it's empty.

III

JOHN SMITH

"There was a child went forth every day,
And the first object he look'd upon,
that object he became ..."
– Walt Whitman

Here are the phrases people most often use to describe me
– "She is looking for her identity"; "She is torn among several
identities" ...

No. Actually I'm fine, thanks. However, the fact that I've
occupied a number of different squares on the identity chess-
board has helped me to see the fictive nature of identity in
general, and to avoid a few of its pitfalls (racism, patriotic
pride, megalomania, and so forth). True, it has also made me
fragile, because fictions (as has been seen) confer real
strengths; people who are *too* divided, too multiple (like
Romain Gary) run the risk of vertigo, dissociation, suicide.

All the same, you might insist, being a bilingual, pluri-confessional, expat novelist, you can hardly claim to be typical!

Fine. Let's look at a case more typical than my own.

Here is a man named John Smith. He is neither what we call real (he never existed, historically speaking) nor what we call fictional (he is the character of no novel) – let us simply say that he is *plausible*.

In hopes of showing to just what extent, in our species, the border between fiction and reality is permeable, I shall make a thumbnail sketch of this man's life story.

Here we go: a human being.

Shortly after his conception in the state of Kentucky, his parents, Mr. and Mrs. Smith (though the latter once bore a different name), made an appointment for an ultra-sound scan. Upon hearing the doctor exclaim, "It's a boy!" they decided to call him John (in memory of one of the father's favourite uncles), purchased a large quantity of blue baby-clothes, and began to fantasize about his future.

Mr. and Mrs. Smith took pride in being white, Christian, and American; they were thrilled at the idea of having a son; very naturally, they planned to teach him to take pride in the same things as they did.

Little John was born on August 15th, 1980, which also happened to be his Aunt Susie's birthday! "No mere coincidence," of course.

The minute he slithered out of his mother's vagina, people started hugging and kissing him, talking and singing to him. He was wafted into language.

American English with a Southern drawl was the language in which people first spoke to him and sang him lullabies; never would he learn another. (The Arabic he would hear later in life would be pure gibberish to his ears.)

People pronounced his name – *John, John, little Johnny Jon-Jon darling* – so often that he eventually "got it."

He was introduced to his relatives – "Here's your uncle Tom, your sister Val, your cousin Chip," and so forth. Little by little, he came to grasp the family constellation; he did not have much choice in the matter.

Day by day, his brain absorbed tales of little red riding-hoods and big bad wolves, witches turning frogs into princes, and Jesus turning water into wine, and Clark Kent turning himself into Superman and movie actors turning themselves into presidents of the United States.

All these tales were juxta- and superimposed in his brain; clearly, a great deal of magic went on in the world.

He was taught to pray, to count, to hope, and to apologize, to feel superior to Blacks and inferior to his parents – here again, he did not have much choice.

Being at the mercy of adults, he could only become what those adults put into his head. At the age of three, he was in no position to protest, "Come on, that's a bunch of baloney – water cannot turn into wine! People cannot rise from the dead! Whites are not superior to Blacks!"

At age six, he joined the neighbourhood Boy Scouts. They were divided into teams, each of which bore the name of an animal. Let's say that he ended up in the Foxes. In all their various activities, little John had to strive to help the Foxes beat the Squirrels and the Beavers. In order to do so, he had to bond with his teammates, and convince himself that *his* team was superior.

Similarly, when he started playing baseball a few years

later, John had to bond with the other members of his team and do his best to make the opposing team lose.

Without making any particular effort of his own, John was now included in a large number of networks which used the word we with pride. He believed in all these proud *we's* – how could he do otherwise? They structured his daily life and were incorporated into his neuronal circuits.

In school, John learned the history of the United States of America, and that of no other country on the planet.

He learned it, of course, solely from the point of view of white males.

In his English classes, all the poems, short stories, and play excerpts he was asked to read and think about came from the Anglo-American canon.

In his science classes, he was taught two different "theories" about the history of the human species on the planet Earth – Darwin's (according to which man descended from the ape) and the Bible's (according to which God created the universe in six days, made Eve out of Adam's rib, and so forth).

Neither of these theories was of particular interest to him; as a matter of fact he was bored stiff by school and eager to have done with it.

Before and after school, he watched television anywhere between four and five hours a day. Upon reaching adolescence in 1992, he convinced his parents to buy him a PlayStation; thereafter, he devoted two hours daily to television and two or more to video games.

Fictions poured in him by the thousand. In these fictions, the enemy was always either pre-human (reptilian), post-human (robotic), or both. Invariably, it sought to destroy humanity and therefore had to be destroyed by the hero.

The ear-shattering music, the fast-moving and extraordinarily violent images of these films and games flowed through John's senses and left their imprint in his brain. They set the rhythm for his synapses.

In 1998, he graduated from high school with mediocre grades and got a job making hamburgers at McDonald's. He found the work stultifying, so he let off steam at night by going out drinking with his buddies, though he still attended church on Sundays and still believed in God.

One night he went to a party and met Betty, a woman whose platinum blonde hair reminded him of the cyber-heroine Lara Croft. When he came on to her, she responded. He offered to drive her home after the party, managed to make love to her in spite of the steering-wheel, and accidentally got her pregnant.

The four parents insisted that he marry her.

The wedding took place in church. When their child was born some eight months later, John and Betty set about initiating it into the English language, the superiority of Whites over Blacks, Little Red Riding Hood, the Jedi, Spider-Man, Pokémon, and so forth.

To support his family, John took on a better-paying job in a spare parts factory. Even with this raise in salary, however, the couple often found it hard to make ends meet. They tended to be late in paying the rent, and Betty complained about not being able to dress like the women in magazines.

They muddled along in this way for a number of years, feeling that their lives were in a rut and quarrelling frequently.

Occasionally, John cheated on Betty.

During his one-night stands with other women or his visits to prostitutes, he felt almost as virile as the Rambo in his brain; afterwards, however, the Jesus in his brain made him feel guilty.

In the fall of 2002, he downloaded *America's Army*, the thrilling new video game put on line free of charge by the recruitment section of U.S. military, described by its inventor as a "weapon of mass distraction." When America invaded Iraq in the spring of 2003, John decided to sign up, kissed his wife and son good-bye, and went off to California to do his basic training.

In Fort Sill, he found himself in an enormous "synthetic theatre of war" co-devised by the Pentagon, Windows, and Hollywood film studios. After a month of immersion in this virtual, interactive, multisensorial environment, he flew off to Baghdad.

He had no idea where Iraq was, and was not even motivated to punish those "Arab bastards" who had brought down the Twin Towers on 9/11. All he cared about was the salary, the intoxicating dream of heroism, and the change of air.

Let's say he was part of the 101st Infantry battalion. Before long, he and his platoon-mates (who hailed from

twenty different states, and most of whom were black)
began to see blood and to hear explosions.

He was terrified of the Iraqis – who spoke gibberish,
wished him dead, were swarthy-skinned, shifty, and un-
Christian. He began to hate them. Mutually reinforcing, his
fear and hatred sent adrenalin shooting through his veins. As
he fought in the streets of Baghdad, the headphones in his
helmet blared heavy metal music into his ears – his favourite
piece was "Bloodflower" by The Cure.

One day he received a bullet in the back and fell down
dead. His corpse was shipped back to the United States,
and his parents wept as it was placed into a casket and low-
ered into the ground. His mother consoled herself with the
idea that she would meet up with him in Heaven someday,
and that God must have had His reasons for calling John
back to His side.

John Smith was posthumously awarded a number of
military medals and decorations for his unusual courage.

His tombstone was covered with flowers.

So ends the tale of an ordinary man – a man whose life
on Earth (though he didn't know it) was made up almost
exclusively of fictions.

If, dear reader, you happen to be an American, this tale may not seem grotesque to you. To perceive the grotesquery, all you need to do is transpose it abroad: imagine, for instance, the tale of a typical Frenchman named Jacques Dupont, a kid from the sticks of Central France who got himself killed in the Algerian War after having been inculcated with French fictions from "Our Ancestors the Gauls" to Brigitte Bardot and the Virgin of Lourdes. ... Ah! Now it looks like fiction?

IV

THE STORYTELLING BRAIN

"I speak of dreams, the offspring of idle brains..."
— W. Shakespeare

Our belief in our selves is virtually impossible to shake. (That is what Buddhist monks spend their lives trying to do ...)

The *I* is a self-perpetuating illusion; as a rule, it prefers to register only those impressions which corroborate and reinforce its sense of its own existence.

We treat little babies as if they were *I*'s that had not yet learned to express themselves, whereas the cerebral synapses that will later make up their I are not in place yet. We treat senile elders as if they had relapsed into childhood, whereas the cerebral synapses that were keeping their selves in place have come undone.

In their normal state, unbeknownst to us, our brains are involved in a number of perfectly astonishing activities.

Here as elsewhere, studying abnormality can help us to understand normality ...

The Divided Brain

In patients suffering from acute epilepsy, before medication was developed to prevent the transmission of seizures from one half of the brain to the other, the *corpus callosum* connecting the two would sometimes be surgically severed. Thus, the two hemispheres could no longer communicate with one another. As is well known, only the left hemisphere (in right-handed people, and in many who are left-handed as well) can consciously record verbal information.

In the 1980s, psychologist Michael Gazzaniga carried out a number of fascinating experiments with these "callotomized" patients, as they were called. In one, the patient was asked to stare intently at the centre of a screen. Shortly afterwards, the word *Walk* was flashed onto the left side of the screen. The message was picked up by the left eye and transmitted to the right brain, which read and understood it, but could not communicate its meaning to the verbalizing left brain. The patient stood up and headed for the door. "Where are you going?" asked the doctor. "I'm thirsty," replied the patient unhesitatingly. "I'm going to buy myself a Coke."

Since he had moved towards the door, he must have had a motivation for doing so; thirst was a plausible motivation; the left brain came up with this hypothesis in the twinkling of an eye and suggested it to the patient, who received and treated it as if it were the truth.

He was not lying, for he firmly believed what he had said. He was confabulating.

All of us confabulate in this manner, in all good faith, without knowing it.

Sometimes we can "sneak up" on our brains, as it were, and watch them in the act of spinning tales for us to believe in.

The other day, for instance, I entered my building, saw that the elevator was stopped on one of the upper floors, heard someone enter it and start heading down. When the doors opened on the ground floor, I expected to see one of my neighbours emerge, which is what always happens in this situation. Not today, however. (Now I must make it clear that all the mental processes described in the following paragraph took place within a few milliseconds.)

At eye level, I saw nothing; disconcerted, I thought, oh, it's not an adult, it must be a small child; glancing downward, I saw that I was wrong – it was a woman, but her head was at my waist level. She's defecating, I thought. ... No, she's shinnying up from an underground tunnel through a hole in the elevator floor. ... No, she had to crouch down to rummage through her handbag for a key.

What is important here is that my brain did not first record my neighbour's unusual posture and *then* go on to speculate as to the reasons for it. It came up with three different answers – two wrong and one right – before it had so much as asked itself a question.

The recording of reality does not precede its interpretation; the two are simultaneous.

We humans are *incapable* of not searching for Meaning. It is an irresistible impulse.

The Damaged Brain
Here is another striking example drawn from my personal experience. Last year, due to complications following internal

surgery, my father spent a few hours in a coma and suffered minor brain damage due to hypoxia (lack of oxygen). Some patients who endure similar damage become amnesiac. In my father, the result was exactly the opposite – rather than losing memories, he began to manufacture them.

His doctors used the word *déjà-vu* to label the symptom. However, far from being rare and fleeting like those "uncanny" feelings of familiarity all of us have from time to time, my father's *déjà-vu*s were continual, coherent, and – especially – *convincing*. His false memories were so vivid and detailed that he could not distinguish them from the real ones. They seriously disrupted his daily life.

No matter what we said to him, he was convinced that he'd already heard it.

No matter what activity we suggested, he felt certain that he'd already done it.

"How about a game of crib?" I said to him one morning. "Sure," he responded at once. "You gave me such a whopping yesterday, I have to take my revenge." Not only had we not played crib the day before, it had been a couple of years since our last game. My suggestion had sparked off the *image* of a card game in his brain, and instead of projecting this image into the future, he had projected it into the past. Its disguise was so perfect that he was unable to distinguish it from his real memories.

We sat down and started to play. My father did fine, sizing up his hands perhaps a bit more slowly than before his operation, but as accurately as ever. Coming across a three of clubs with the top right-hand corner broken off, he exclaimed, "Look, you *must* remember! Yesterday you slammed all the clubs down so hard that you broke the corner off the three!"

From the outside, though disconcerting, there was something comical about these false memories. They reminded me of children's fibs – "No, it's not my fault, it's because ..." – fibs they insist upon so hotly that they end up believing them.

From my father's point of view, however, what was going on was anything but funny. He found it upsetting to be challenged by his friends and family, several dozen times a day, as to the veracity of events he was convinced he had experienced a few hours or a few days earlier.

The following day, my stepmother and I took him to the hospital for a series of tests. As my stepmother went off to get the wheelchair, I helped my father out of the car.

Suddenly, he turned to me and said, "I hope you are not going to trick me the way you did the other day, grabbing the wheelchair and zooming all over the parking lot while I stand here leaning on my cane!" Needless to say, there had been no "other day"; this was the first time I had accompanied them to the hospital. Again, he had shot a sort of movie in his mind ("Nancy might run off with the wheelchair ...") – and then, instantaneously and involuntarily, stored the movie among his memories.

On a Sunday afternoon, I went out for a walk in a nearby forest with one of my half-brothers, his wife, and their toddler. After an hour or so, we got lost. We hadn't brought a compass with us, and because the sky was cloudy we could not orient ourselves by the sun. It started getting dark. We got bogged down in marshes and had to teeter our way across them on bobbing, slippery logs, the three adults passing the child from hand to hand. When we finally got home, exhausted and relieved, we told my father about our exciting adventure. Again, as each of the episodes passed our lips – the darkening sky, the slippery logs, the way we had handed the child to each other across the marsh – he was adamant: he already knew every detail of the story by heart.

My father's condition has since improved, but just imagine the distress of patients who suffer permanently from this syndrome! When they go shopping, they're unable to purchase anything; the minute they see a product on the shelf, they're convinced they've already bought it. When they surf channels on television, all the films, mini-series, news programs and documentaries seem hopelessly familiar to them ...

Their brains are taking them for a ride.

Ours do the same. A flagrant example is what neurologists call saccades. Several times per second, our eyes "jump," briefly interrupting their recording of the world so as to smooth out our brain's reception of it. Since our head level changes constantly as we walk, without saccades our vision would bob up and down – much like what we see on the screen during "hand-held camera" sequences! Being designed for the express purpose of going unnoticed, however, the tall tales normal brains tell their owners do not draw attention to themselves.

A major exception: dreams.

The Idle Brain
Throughout his convalescence, my father's dreams were extremely colourful and vivid. Only in the morning, as he told them to us over breakfast, did he talk with any degree of confidence – at least no one could challenge the content

of his dreams! I bought him a tape recorder so that he could record them, and he did so with great diligence.

Occasionally, his false memories would give rise to dreams, or the other way around (it was impossible to say which).

After my return to France, he told me over the phone that he wanted to share one of his recent dreams with me. "I was in an enormous gym. Every element in it was connected to you, and to the conversation we'd had the other day. You had said that gyms should have different-coloured walls. Well, this one did – they were green, purple, deep maroon. ... It was an absolutely amazing structure, with basketball courts, a swimming pool, high ceilings, and flowers everywhere, cascades of flowers with no scent, but no insects either. ... There were sofas overflowing with cushions; it made you want to get down on the floor and roll around on them. ... The whole thing was just *exalting*, and I wanted to share some of that excitement with you."

Deeply moved, I decided not to upset my father by "correcting" his perceptions yet again – there had been no such conversation between us, and I had never given much thought to the interior decoration of gymnasiums (though it did occur to me that, spelled differently, "gym" was my father's given name). ...

Yes, dream narratives are also confabulations.

Take the following experience, which most inhabitants of the modern Western world have probably had at least once: in the course of a lengthy, complicated dream, the doorbell rings or a police siren starts to wail. ... When you wake up, you realize that it was in fact your alarm clock ringing. You scratch your head incredulously – how could your alarm clock have gone off at exactly the right moment in your dream?

The answer to this question is the same as for my father's *déjà-vus*: our brains are taking us for a ride. *The impression we have, and which we feel to be utterly and completely true, is false.* The truth is that our brain concocted the entire dream narrative when the alarm clock went off, thus allowing us to prolong our sleep by a few seconds.

Just as the callotomized patient, in saying, "I'm going to buy myself a Coke," made up a story to explain the fact that he was heading for the door, and just as my father, in saying, "You slammed all the clubs down!" made up a story to explain the card with the broken corner, so all of us, in saying, "I dreamed I was being chased by a police car," make up a story to explain the sound of the alarm clock.

What is Meaningful is not the dream, it is the dream narrative, which is already an interpretation.

Just *because* dreams have no Meaning in and of themselves (any more than life does), dream narratives, like childhood memories, can help psychoanalysts study the ways in which each of us fabricates Meaning.

We can only feel sorry for the dogmatic shrinks who, given this infinitely rich material, reduce all childhood memories to the Oedipal complex, and all dream mechanisms to pan-sexualism. We can especially feel sorry for their patients!

The amazing truth is that to this day, no scientist worthy of the name has been able to come up with a convincing hypothesis as to why, in the course of the evolution of the higher animal species on planet Earth, dreams appeared.

Yes, all birds and mammals dream (with a single, delightful exception – the duck-billed platypus!).

Even opossums dream, and they are "fossile" animals that have existed on the North American continent for the past 180 million years. What dark, unconscious wishes might the dreams of a baby opossum be trying to express?

"Chickens dream of grain," as the Talmud put it!

* * *

Dreams, Shakespeare tells us, are *the offspring of an idle brain.*

Contemporary neurologists agree: during "paradoxical sleep" – those four or five twenty-minute periods nightly during which we dream actively and have rapid eye movements – some regions of the brain are at rest and some synapses disconnected, while other regions and synapses continue to function. No longer being coordinated by the centralizing, fully conscious "I," they churn up contents virtually at random – traces of the day's events, images that have made an impression on us, wisps of memory, and so forth.

The stories get told, in other words, not by the dreams themselves but by the brain. The minute we wake up, with no solicitation on our part, our brains spontaneously *turn* our dreams into stories, then go on to speculate as to their meaning. No wonder we find those "meanings" mysterious!

It is really rather mind-boggling, when you think about it. Even a damaged brain, one that has lost a part of its diurnal coherency, goes on spinning incredible tales for us, based on our nocturnal images. The narrative mechanism innate to the human brain goes on combining and organizing. ... It insists on enchanting us, disturbing us, casting a spell upon us – pulling us back, again and again, into the human world, which is the world of fictions.

No political regime could ever succeed in controlling our tale-telling. Even were we to follow the example of Plato's *Republic* and banish poets and playwrights from our societies, no tyrant, dictator, monarch, or president could ever eliminate our dreams, nightmares, fantasies, and deliriums – all the feverish activity through which our brains perpetually manufacture stories *and believe in them*, so that our time on Earth will be not merely an existence but a life – that is, something which appears to follow a path, reflect a destiny, contain a Meaning.

The irrepressible storytelling brain is what makes us human. As we shall see in the upcoming chapters, however, the word *human* is not necessarily a compliment.

V

HEADING FOR THE UR-TEXT

"No doubt discovered before fire, fiction was born in the network of our neurones at the same time as words and gestures. Oral for eons before it finally got committed to writing and, later still, printed, it served from the outset to disguise our ignorance of our origins, quell our fears of the inexplicable, and justify the power wielded over the many by the craftier, wilier few. Much of this remains with us even today ..."
– Hubert Nyssen

Human language, as opposed to computer language, can apprehend reality only by lending it Meaning – a Meaning favourable, as a general rule, to the person who is talking.

This is original sin, if you wish, except that since it is involuntary the word *sin* is inappropriate. More accurately, this is humanity's *built-in bug* – the storytelling brain that turns us now into angels, now into devils.

Outside of humanity, of course, there are neither angels nor devils.

* * *

We humans find it virtually impossible to acknowledge that *there is no particular merit in being born this or that.*

To be born, for a human, is to *deserve* to be born.

Among illiterate peoples, genealogy (no matter how fanciful) is the primary element of education – that is, of identity.

As of our conception (psychic before physical – the *dream* of a child conceived by its mother, its father, or both), we are endowed with an artificial merit – that of being "the child of So-and-so."

The fictions start there, and do not stop until we have been effaced from the memory of all the living.

A tiny human child can be taught to speak any language, sing any tune, appreciate any food, believe in any god.

The human mind is like a wax record in which grooves are etched more or less deeply. The first imprints – mother tongue, fairy and folk tales, songs, visual, olfactory and gustatory impressions – are the deepest ones. As has been seen, it is with them, *through* them, that our synapses get broken in, our cerebral circuits set up. They are the very material of our selves.

Babies have no critical distance. The first impressions bond us to our parents though they be torturers, and make us wary of others though they be saints.

It is impossible to overestimate the importance of the grooves etched during the first six years of our lives. Whereas "we" are not yet there to be aware of it, they shape our most powerful emotions – located in that part of the brain we shall later come to think of as our "guts." (This is the part that will be reactivated later on in life, when we sob as we listen to a particular piece of music, or feel the urge to rape a child.)

The sum total of these first impressions is what is known as our *culture*. For each and all of us, it will be the world itself.

* * *

To welcome a child into the world is to make a place for it within a series of concentric circles: family / ethnic group / church / clan / tribe / country, and so forth.

Before it can say *I*, it needs to exist within a series of we's. Invariably, the latter are defined by contrast with a series of more or less threatening thems.

You are one of us. The others are the enemy. This is the archaic, all-powerful Ur-text of the human species, the basic structure of all primitive narratives, from caveman lore to *Star Wars*.

To put it tautologically, a group is a group. For the sake of its cohesion and survival, it will spontaneously tend to think of itself as *the* group, and to interiorize its culture as the culture. When elements from other cultures come along, they will automatically be compared and contrasted with those of the first.

Like all primates only more so, being a fragile and threatened species, humans learned to survive by identifying powerfully with an *us* and perceiving all *them*'s as enemies.

Yes: life is tough, and we are afraid. Fear is the normal

response of all animals to the prospect of death, but the fact that humans know about their deaths in advance changes everything.

In a word, it makes our species paranoid.

Paranoia, the pathology of *overinterpretation*, is mankind's congenital illness.

In the days of our ancient ancestors, this paranoid structure was probably indispensable. In recent decades, it has become seriously counterproductive. Being hardwired into our cerebral circuits, however, it is still very much with us.

* * *

Primitive peoples are convinced that everything occurs for a reason (the hand of God, the malevolence of neighbours or spirits, and so forth).

There are any number of primitives in the modern Western world. "I don't believe in chance," they say, for instance. "There's no such thing as chance" ... "The invisible hand" ... "The stratagem of History" ... "Reality is rational" ... All of these statements are religious, magical.

"I don't believe in chance": an excellent summary of human history.

Humans interpret everything, and their quintessential interpretation goes like this: if I've got a problem, someone must have wished it on me.

What do superstitious peasants do when illness decimates their livestock? What do the residents of Soweto do when one of them shows symptoms of HIV? They interpret these events as magical attacks. *Who* cast a spell on me? How can I undo this spell?

They feel justified in undertaking costly, complex ceremonies to placate ancestors and spirits – gestures which, scientifically speaking, have no connection whatsoever to the illnesses but which, fictionally speaking, are effective, and especially irrefutable.

If the animals' or the person's health does not improve, they can always decide the remedies were not strong enough, or blame it on a new spell.

In the wake of the 9/11 attacks, the United States behaved like a primitive tribe. *Who* cast a spell on us? How can we undo this spell? Being under threat, they felt justified in undertaking costly, complex military ceremonies that had no connection whatsoever to the attacks.

* * *

How do we survive? By bonding among ourselves and ganging up on others.

Inclusion and exclusion are the primordial functions of human stories.

We's are created and reinforced by concocting, telling, and retelling the story of their collective past. They depend on memory, that is, on fiction. Pride is the bond, the cement. All *we*'s strive to be proud of what they are. They need to do so – for the security and serenity of the *I*'s who make them up.

People who can find nothing to be proud of in the various we's to which they belong can go berserk.

Imagine, for instance, what would happen if large numbers of poor, swarthy Muslim workers were to immigrate to a country whose population was predominantly wealthy, white, and Christian or non-religious, and their children were unable to take pride in *either* their ancestors or the inhabitants of the land of their birth and citizenship: this would be a potentially explosive situation.

The tricky thing with pride is getting the dosage right. Too much can lead to violence, but so can too little.

Violence is also cherished in and of itself, for it creates events, that is, stories, that is, Meaning.

Even today, in many parts of the world, adults convey the following message to their children: we alone are truly human, speak a true language, and have a true history. Other people tell other stories (basically nonsense, or blasphemy) in other languages (basically gibberish).

To be frightened, mistrustful, and on guard, to rise up against our enemies, to defend ourselves by attacking, to tell stories in which the valorous we confront the threatening *them* and emerge victorious from the confrontation – this is the blahblah that has enabled our species to survive.

Chimpanzees also live in bands for protection, and feel the pride of belonging; they do not, however, spend their time reciting their genealogies or recounting the tales of their past heroic battles.

In the Western world, initiation into humanity takes

place through lullabies, television cartoons, fairy-tales, fables, myths and religious parables, video games, documentary films, history classes. All these narratives are based on artificial coherence and have similar structures.

Of its own history and the history of others, each country tells the version it finds the most gratifying, the one that shows it in the most flattering light. Many important facts get condemned to oblivion and vanish forever; others, on the contrary, solidify into official fictions and are ceaselessly emphasized, commemorated, taught.

What is the "true" story of your family, or your country? You don't have the faintest idea – and for good reason.

What we are taught about our Nation, our family line, and so forth, is not reality but fiction. The facts have been meticulously selected and organized so as to make up a coherent, edifying tale. What happened to the duds, the whores, the halfwits, the wrongdoings, the massacres, the tragic mistakes?

All historical narratives are fictional because they tell only part of the story. Only God could tell the whole story. Unfortunately, being outside of Time, God cannot tell stories.

An intensive study was once made of the ways in which the discovery / conquest / invasion / colonization of the New World was narrated in the school textbooks of seventy different countries. The study makes edifying reading. No two versions are alike.

This does not mean that facts do not exist; it means that human beings are unable to apprehend and transmit facts without interpreting them.

Millions of inhabitants of the New World indeed lost their lives as a result of the arrival of a few thousand Europeans; millions of Africans were indeed deported and sold as slaves. However, the minds of the actors of these situations were filled with fictions that served to explain what was happening to them, or to justify what they were doing. The Aztecs believed the Spaniards to be gods; the Spaniards believed they were legitimately extending their king's dominion or spreading the word of Christ; fair-skinned men saw themselves as the natural masters of dark-skinned men, and so forth.

Six million Jews indeed perished in the Nazi concentration and death camps, but they perished because of a bad fiction – namely, the natural superiority of the Aryan race. Once dead, they could be reinserted into other bad fictions

– the one, for example, about *a land without people and a people without a land, or the one about a Return*, which gives every Jew in the world – even recent converts, half-Jews and Falashas, even those Jews none of whose traceable ancestors ever lived in Palestine or so much as heard the word *Palestine* – to come to Israel/Palestine and settle permanently there.

Bonobos do not teach their children: between 1939 and 1945, those guys almost succeeded in wiping us off the face of the earth; never forget it; because of that tragedy we now have the right to live here; in 1948, those people chased us off our land and took it over; never forget it; they deserve to be pushed into the sea.

Blowing one's own horn is humanity's favourite music.

Nowhere in the world, perhaps, is the fictive nature of human identities more evident than in the city of Jerusalem, where they are madly juxta- and superimposed. The city resembles a gigantic Monopoly or Lego game handed out to the various groups with no instructions for use, so that each has undertaken in its own way to define the rules, determine the Meaning of the different pieces, decide who is the winner, who the loser, and how the game should "inexorably" unfold.

Today, any African-American in the United States, any Jew or Muslim living in the Middle East, could theoretically say to himself or herself, "Okay, I've had it. From now on, I'm going to be free and autonomous. My people's heritage, with its heroic sacrifices and monumental tragedies, is no longer of any concern to me. I refuse to be determined by the past, passively dependent on what happened to my ancestors. From now on, like the hero of a novel by Sartre or Kundera, I will forge my own destiny."

If they do not make this decision, it's because it would damage the fictional foundations of their being – fidelity towards their parents, ancestors or coreligionaries; identification with their suffering; need to pass on their stories.

If they *do* make this decision, however, they will be free only to subscribe to another fiction – the childish, arrogant, Promethean fiction of the self-engendered, self-sufficient individual.

* * *

As the story of John Smith shows, children are at the mercy of the fictions inculcated into them by adults. They have no choice but to take them seriously, especially when their parents seem to consider them sacred.

These fictions are always biased, almost always simplistic, and often dangerous.

Since our brains do not contain hermetically sealed chambers, one for fantasy and another for reality, children intermingle and superimpose facts and fictions. What they learn about real kings is coloured by what they know about fairy-tale kings. What they are told about God the Father influences their perception of their own fathers, and vice versa.

Only much later – and even then, only if they are lucky – will they learn to think for themselves and challenge some of the fictions they ingested at an early age.

What do I mean by "lucky"?

Lucky people are those who have access to other cultures. The fictional nature of the latter being instantly apparent to them, it can help them grasp the fictional nature of their own. The luckiest people of all are those who have access to the *novels* of other cultures.

Ayaan Hirsi Ali, raised by a Somalian mother who practised a repressive, dogmatic version of Islam, was lucky enough to live in four different countries before the age of twenty; this can only have whetted her intelligence. She underwent a real inner revolution when, in the Kenyan school she attended as an adolescent, she started reading English and American novels. In her autobiography *Infidel*, she says that Robert Louis Stevenson's *Dr. Jekyll and Mr. Hyde* had an especially powerful impact on her – because, unlike the Manichean religious fictions she had been taught up until then, it helped her to see that good and evil could exist within a single individual.

The vast majority of human children do not have this good fortune.

John Smith didn't have it. Little boys who get sent to Koranic schools in Afghanistan don't have it. Nor do little girls in North Korea, who learn to dance and sing the praises of Kim Jong-Il. And so forth.

* * *

The human brain's innate penchant for narrativity, knowingly manipulated by religious discourse over the centuries, has in recent years begun to be exploited by the media, governments, big business, and the military.

The buzzword for this process is *storytelling*. "Facts talk," as a cynical specialist put it, "but stories sell."

Under a thousand different guises – in the workplace, in our city streets, on our television and computer screens – stories are presented to us as "true" and we are asked to adhere to them, believe in them, be moved and inspired by them, identify with their characters, implicate ourselves in their plots and morals.

Propaganda; disinformation. Because of the emotions elicited in us by these simple, edifying tales, we can easily be persuaded to buy such-and-such a product, vote for such-and-such a candidate, commit ourselves to such-and-such a company, support such-and-such a cause.

Sweetened with storytelling, lies are amazingly easy to swallow.

* * *

To be civilized is to recognize that identity is a con-struction, become acquainted with numerous texts – and, through them, learn to identify with people unlike oneself.

Unfortunately, no matter how sophisticated we are, it is always possible – no, easy – to reactivate our gut fears. Try carrying out the following experiment, in all honesty: the next time you are very hungry or very frightened, observe your behaviour. In all likelihood, your spontaneous tendency will be to become suspicious of those around you and to blame them for your misery. This is what nations do.

Whenever a nation feels threatened or humiliated (like Germany after the Treaty of Versailles or the United States after the World Trade Center attacks), it will spontaneously – and dangerously – tend to revert to the Ur-text.

Bad fictions give rise to hatred, wars, and massacres. People are willing to torture, kill, or die for bad fictions.

It happens every day.

VI

BELIEFS

*"Whenever Man cuts himself off from myths in the
name of realism, he turns into a pile of meat."*
– Romain Gary

To recapitulate: for bonobos and chimpanzees, reality suffices; they derive meaning from it.

Humans, on the other hand, require something *above
and beyond*, underlying, overarching reality: this is
Meaning.

Monkeys take into account the alternation between day
and night; only humans interpret it.

Apollo, they say, for instance. Or: *The Great Tortoise. Or: Ra, the Sun God.* Or: *Our Lord in His infinite mercy.* They say all sorts of things, tell all sorts of stories, invent all sorts of chimeras.

This is how we humans see the world – by saying it, i.e, by interpreting it, i.e., by inventing it. Because we are fragile – far more fragile than any of the other large primates.

Our imagination compensates for our fragility by giving reality a Meaning it does not have in and of itself. Without our imagination, we should have vanished from the surface of the earth – just as the dinosaurs did.

* * *

The human self cannot help extrapolating. Gaily and involuntarily, it projects itself backwards and forwards in time, imagining that it has always existed and is destined to exist forever. Believing in its own immortality comes *naturally* to it.

Touching, isn't it?

It's also false, but that is hardly worth mentioning.

Heaven, Hell, the immortality of the soul, meeting up with one's loved ones in the Great Beyond or the Great Hereafter – all this is claptrap, if you like: but it is claptrap endowed with the formidable power – the formidable *reality* – of the imagination.

It *effectively* helps people to live, to endure the pain of loss, to mourn, to renew their energies for the day to come.

Thus, it is impossible to say that God does not exist.

All we can say is that He does not exist outside of human minds. But to exist to *that extent*, in *so many* human minds, is a prodigious amount of existence indeed!

What exists in human minds truly exists. Just look at the results!

Impressive, to say the least.

In Europe, they run the gamut from marvels (Bach, Michelangelo, etc.) to massacres (Crusades, religious wars, etc.).

In Africa and Polynesia: when a religious leader puts on a frightening mask representing a particular spirit or god of war, he temporarily becomes that spirit, and this gives him genuine power.

In Haiti, in Brazil, in Arabia: during their trances and dances, voodoo adepts and whirling dervishes possessed by gods or spirits perform feats of physical prowess and endurance of which they would be incapable in their normal state.

The faith billions of people place in a transcendent reality inspires, supports, *and transforms* them, day after day.

It can incite them to help the poor, or to fasten a bomb around their waists and blow themselves up in a packed city bus.

In our species, as Rousseau was already aware, the best and the worst flow from the same source.

* * *

To construct an ethics, to organize life in society, people need to see Good and Evil represented.

A visit to Italy: roaming the streets of Parma and Modena, entering churches and museums one after the other, I see the thousands of traces left by the Christian narratives that have helped human beings to make sense of their lives in this part of the world. Nativities, Crucifixions, angels, devils, the martyrdom of saints, the punishment of sinners, Last Judgments ... a vast panorama of characters in whom millions of individuals have recognized themselves, and through whom they have communed.

Countless European paintings and sculptures depict pain, horror, torture, and cruelty. When these evils are inflicted on the good guys (the saints, for instance, or Christ himself), believers murmur, *How dreadful!*; when they are inflicted upon the bad guys, they murmur, *Hah! Serves them right!* This helps to confer Meaning on their own, inevitable suffering.

A visit to India: in Delhi, Jaipur, Mumbai, I see a whole *different* panorama of characters, drawn not from the monotheistic Gospel tales, but from the polytheistic Hindu ones contained in the *Mahabharata* and the *Ramayana*. Their function, however, is identical.

In the Jewish and Muslim worlds, where images of living beings are theoretically proscribed, believers are encouraged to identify with Good and to reject Evil through the repetition of stories passed down over the centuries.

In Africa, Polynesia, the West Indies, the Amazon, over the entire surface of the Earth, in their incredible diversity but with an irresistible strength, belief in gods, spirits, and ancestors has shaped human minds and cemented human communities.

Even in the atheistic Soviet Union, the government knew that "the masses" could not dispense with this sort of communion. The faces of Marx, Engels, and Lenin replaced those of Jesus and the Virgin Mary as ubiquitous icons, and instead of the lives of the saints, schoolchildren committed to memory the heroic acts of the martyrs of Communism.

No reasoning, philosophy, legal, or executive system, however just and enlightened, can get rid of the tensions, anxieties, and conflicts inherent to the fact that human beings live in time, and know they must die.

One of the weaknesses of public discourse since the Enlightenment is that it wants to deal only with Good.

To be sure, our governments punish evildoers! Unlike religions, however, they prefer to ignore the fact that most people suffer most of the time.

Yes, because life is rough, and it has not gotten any less rough in our part of the world, dominated by Reason, than in those parts "still" subjected to monotheistic or pagan superstitions.

Emancipated from the magical beliefs of their ancestors, modern individuals still need to deal with the unpleasant fact that most of their wishes are not and will never be fulfilled.

Since it is crucial to them that their suffering be Meaningful, enlightenment is not enough; they also need to understand darkness.

To know is not enough; they also need to believe.

This is why, since the eighteenth century, the Western world has witnessed the flowering of an enormous parallel culture that depicts and explores evil and misery – modern art, from the novel to violent video games, gore movies, science fiction, and pornography.

* * *

Man cannot live on bread alone, said Jesus. And he was right: bonobos are the ones who live on bread alone. Man needs *Meaningful* bread.

Faith reinforces each individual's sense of self, and effectively bonds individuals to one another.

Communion, communication, community: all of these things come about when a group of human beings agrees that *this* is the Meaning of life – no matter what the content of the *this*.

Thanks to their agreement, they will comfort and support each other in the name of Christ, Allah, Buddha, and so forth. The comfort and support *truly* exist. Little does it matter that their causes are fictions.

Jesus, Lao Tse, Buddha, and so forth were great wise men. (Perhaps more than any other religion, the original version of Buddhism pointed up the fictional aspects of human existence.) To their wisdom, however, the masses invariably prefer submission, obedience, conformity to norms, rituals, and supersitutions.

Mea culpa, mea culpa, mea maxima culpa. ... More than twenty centuries after the death of Jesus, at the heart of the European continent, people still pronounce these words with fervour in church every Sunday. Human beings want to feel guilty ... but not too responsible. This is why submission is a far more powerful penchant than freedom.

Acknowledging that we cannot control everything is but a step away from abdicating our wills – a step many people take with a sense of relief.

Heaven and Hell. ... These, too, are fictions – and we might be justified in feeling indignant about them. So many millions of pages wasted on false hopes and fears! So many thundering sermons inflicted on terrified congregations! So many lives spent vainly hoping ... for *nothing*!

And yet it was not for nothing, because those hopes and fears conferred Meaning upon millions of lives. That was all they were meant to do.

In North America, born-again Christians invite Jesus into their hearts and ask him to run their lives for them. They count upon him to console them, to reassure them, and to make all their difficult decisions for them. He never lets them down.

Yes, all of these fictions truly help people live their lives. "Faith," as Douglas Kennedy says, "is perhaps the most important impulse in life – the fundamental means by which a vast majority of people get through the day."

Opium of the people? If you like ... except that there is no such thing as a people without opium.

Drugs, religion, politics, love. ... Countless "opiums" help human beings structure their inner reality harmoniously and convincingly, thus enabling them to believe in themselves, to act in the world, and to value their own existence in it.

We should put an end to all this silliness? Fine – but how? No gulag could ever be big enough. ...

* * *

We can deplore the resignation of believers, their fatalism: ("We are in God's hands"; "Everything that happens has been willed by Allah") ...

Over the past century and a half, geneticians and sociobiologists have been teaching us about another sort of fatality. The fact is, they tell us, that there is nothing but determinism, chance, and the infinitely unpredictable interaction between the two.

The problem is that humans can only survive in societies, and that it is impossible to erect a society upon that sort of *fact*.

"We are in God's hands" is a much more solid foundation!

Religious leaders tell stories; geneticians do not.

Explanations need to do two things: firstly, provide us with a model of reality, and secondly, convince us. Undeniably, the scientific approach "beats" the religious approach for the first aspect – but not for the second!

We no longer explain mental illness in terms of possession by the devil, magic spells, or an imbalance of bodily "humours." Applying a different interpretive system, we now tend to seek the reasons for people's insanity in their "family romances."

True, as compared to the religious approach, the Freudian approach has the advantage of *knowingly* stimulating our interpretative machinery. It recognizes the self as a construction, and attempts to grasp – through what we say about our dreams, our childhood, our difficulties, and our syndromes – what went awry in the fabrication of that self.

For all that, nothing guarantees that after ten years on the couch, the patient will be feeling any better than the adept of a religious sect or the fanatic of a political cause.

Moreover, psychoanalysis is vulnerable to the same defects as religions: abuse of power, personality cult, dogmatism, servility, superstition, absurd ritual. In the minds of many psychotherapists, the Unconscious plays exactly the same role as God in the minds of believers – it explains everything!

All explanations in which people believe *effectively* confer Meaning on their lives.

* * *

To be Jewish is a fiction.
To be Muslim is a fiction.
To be Christian is a fiction.
To be Hindu is a fiction.
To be a voodoo adept, etc. – all of these things are fictions.

In and of themselves, they are neither good nor bad. On the other hand ...
Good Jews and Bad Muslims: a deleterious fiction.
Good Muslims and Bad Jews: a deleterious fiction.
Good Christians and bad infidels: a deleterious fiction.

Ur-Texts, once again. Wars and massacres guaranteed.

The Good Samaritan: a beneficial fiction. A story which, instead of presenting itself as true, presents itself as a story.

It *contains* a truth – namely, that we can identify with the suffering of people who belong to groups other than our own.

Such is the premise – and the promise – of the novel.

Polytheisms, monotheisms, even nihilisms: so many confabulations that give human beings a handle on their earthly existence.

They are not true, but to the extent that their adepts believe in them, and behave in accordance with that belief, they are *effective*.

Thus, there are two sorts of truth: the *objective* sort, whose results can be confronted with reality (sciences, techniques, daily life), and the *subjective* sort, which can only be attained through inner experience (myths, religions, literature).

No religion can provide us with an objective answer to the question of why the universe and mankind exist. All of them, on the other hand, provide excellent subjective answers.

Believing in unreal things helps people to endure real life.

VII

WAR FABLES

"We really must be living for nothing, dear Lord,
to be forever reduced to dying for something."
– Romain Gary

That we are born and must die: such is the perpetual gripe of human beings. Job, Beckett, all of us.

Job: "Why didst thou bring me forth from the womb? / Would that I had died before any eye had seen me, / and were as though I had not been, / carried from the womb to the grave."

Beckett: "Women give birth astride the tomb."

All of us: "Where was I before I was born, Mommy? Why does everyone have to die, Daddy?"

The other animals do not wonder about these things. They experience birth and death, unaware that they were born and will die.

Whence the inexhaustible human obsession with sexuality (which can lead to birth), violence (which can lead to death), and every conceivable interaction between the two.

What makes our species unique is not that it has been waging war from time immemorial (chimpanzees and ants can claim as much), but that it turns its wars into History ... and millions of stories.

If you replace the word war with the word love in the preceding sentence, it will be equally true. How does confabulation work in these two vast domains?

* * *

In peacetime, it is often very hard for people to find Meaning in their lives.

Despite all the tragedies it causes, war is desirable (and desired) because it reactivates the Ur-text, thus injecting a huge dose of Meaning into the lives of those who wage it and those who endure it. (It is a well-known fact that suicide rates plunge in wartime.) The war "theatre," as it is aptly called, is one of the greatest purveyors of Meaning invented by our species.

The Meaning is both aesthetic and ethical.

Aesthetically: the forms and rituals of the military institution – parades and uniforms, the choreography of weapons deployment, the staging of battles – are even more impressive and spectacular than religious rituals. The battles themselves provide us with mind-boggling scenes: pyrotechnic displays, nuclear mushrooms several miles high, whole cities in flames.

Ethically: through brotherhood-in-arms, the bonding of people faced with a common enemy, the enhancement of love by separation and fear, explosions, surprises, sacrifices, terror, murder, massive loss, screams of enthusiasm and wails of mourning, war reiterates and reinforces moral values and guarantees a maximum intensity of emotion.

By whetting our hatred, war ushers us into a world of striking contrasts. No other phenomenon fosters such a dramatic juxtaposition of extremes.

At first: hundreds of thousands of men who have been trained, drilled, and dressed to the hilt, line up, advance in perfect unison, goose-step, left, right, salute – their every gesture as impeccably coordinated as those of classical ballet dancers – accompanied by shiny new tanks, planes performing breathtaking acrobatics in the air, the metallic perfection of bombs, icy mathematical caluclations, impeccable battle plans.

A while later: cities burned to the ground, crumbled homes and buildings, mountains of debris, poisoned land, a chaos of mutilated, torn, and crushed bodies, emitting all sorts of liquids, tears, piss, shit, vomit, rivers of blood, with their faces ripped off, their intestines tumbling out, bits of flesh and bone mingling with mud.

Later still: medals, statues, monuments, more parades to commemorate our victory, more rituals to honour those who made the ultimate sacrifice, more epic poems to record these crucial events of our collective existence and thus confirm our sense of belonging.

Yes, one of the fundamental purposes of war is to give rise to stories that are thrilling, moving, and *memorable*. We never tire of telling them, watching them, and commenting on them: feature films, documentaries, reportages, the evening news. ...

Without wars, the history of the human species would be singularly lacking in relief, spice, suspense, and sudden developments – in other words, all the elements that go into the making of a good story.

* * *

As far back as you can go in human history, warriors have drawn their inspiration from the tales of other warriors, and bolstered their courage by remembering and reciting the feats of mythical heroes. From Gilgamesh (eighteenth century BC) to Operation Desert Storm (twentieth century CE), war is impossible without myth.

Here again, there is no clearcut distinction between myth and reality. Not only is the imagination a *part* of human reality, it characterizes and produces it.

When we say that 26 million young men lost their lives "for nothing" in the First World War, what we mean is that they died for *bad fictions* – ones which, though their leaders may have believed them, later turned out to be specious, hollow, and untenable ("the Austro-Hungarian Empire," for example).

If a young soldier fighting in Iraq today was raised on tales of Achilles, Napoleon, and Rambo, all of these heroes truly exist in his mind (just as God does). Little does it matter that some of them existed historically and others did not. None is physically present in his brain; all are represented there. Imagining them, however, can give him the real strength he needs to kill real people.

Our thoughts are real. Psychic reality is a powerful and effective reality. Chimeras can kill; thus they are real.

Animals do not function that way.

We need to stop describing people who commit massacres or indulge in orgies as behaving "like animals" or "worse than animals." There is, simply, no comparison.

In war, man *plays* the animal, *acts out* his savagery – animals have no need of this.

No animal commits evil for the sake of evil – or, for that matter, for the sake of good.

Due to the proximity of death, the situation of war can be conducive to sexual arousal. It is possible that, faced with the prospect of their own disappearance, men and women feel the impulse to copulate so as to leave their genes behind them; this could indeed be construed as an "animal" instinct.

There is nothing animalistic, on the other hand, about war rape. Several hundred thousand German women were raped by Russian soldiers during and after the fall of Berlin in May-June of 1945. One of them, a professional journalist then in her early thirties, kept a journal which she later published anonymously. (The book is an extraordinary document – literally so, for, ordinarily, rape victims are too ashamed to tell their stories.) Deprived of leave for long months, the Russian soldiers were certainly starved for sexual contact; even so, their raping of German women was by no means an "instinctive" or self-evident act. It was a symbolic act they felt *obliged* to perform, which is why they did it in front of each other, usually after getting drunk – otherwise, says the anonymous author, they would not have been capable of it.

War rape is a quintessentially human act – it involves attacking, wounding, and punishing the enemy by *spoiling his stories*. The man whose woman has been raped can never again tell himself that she is "pure," that she is "all his," or that her children "belong" to him.

* * *

It is commonly said that warriors dehumanize their enemies, and that executioners dehumanize their victims.

The Nazis, for instance, saw (and treated) Jews like lice; the Hutus saw (and treated) Tutsis like cockroaches.

The critical term here is *like*: the masterword of all fictions.

The Nazis did not believe that the Jews actually *were* lice. They told themselves the following bad fiction: "We need to treat Jews *as if* they were lice because, like lice, they are infecting and spoiling our clean, pure society."

Similarly, the Hutus did not believe that the Tutsis *were* cockroaches. Exalted by the bad fictions pumped into their brains by the broadcasts of Thousand Hills Radio, they said to themselves, "The Tutsis are less numerous but more powerful than we are; that's not fair. They want to take everything away from us; we need to exterminate them as if they were cockroaches."

To be able to treat people like lice or cockroaches, one must first deprive them of their human accoutrements.

This was easy in Auschwitz, where great pains were taken to ensure that the executioners never entered into direct contact with their victims.

It was more difficult in Rwanda, where the massacres entailed one-on-one bodily contact – and where, moreover, the victims were often the neighbours, friends, or even relatives of the executioners. To be able to hack them to pieces with machetes, the Hutus needed to invent a different sort of fiction – i.e., that *it was not really them*.

"True, I'd played soccer with him just the week before," said a young Hutu of a friend he had murdered. "I recognized him. But when I cut him, he wasn't himself. I looked at him and he had a third eye in the middle of his forehead ..."

Recognizing faces and attaching emotion to them take place in two different areas of the brain.

When one of these areas is deactivated, whether because of brain damage or – far more commonly – during sleep, the two functions can be dissociated. In our dreams, we often see an unfamiliar face, but "know" that it's one of our loved ones – or, conversely, like the young Hutu, we see the face of a loved one but "know" that it's really someone else.

The brain is a fabulous machine – one that *predispose*s us to confabulate, for better and for worse.

It provides us with the tales we need to justify our acts.

* * *

What we derive from our sense of belonging (to a family, tribe, nation, gang, etc.) is a *countenance*.

The word *countenance* also means face. All of us gradually construct the face we wish to present to the world; we wear it like a mask and identify with it. Look around you, in any public place – everyone strives to maintain a countenance. It helps us feel that we are coherent, consistent, valid – in a word, that we are "someone." When the mask is torn away, we "lose face"; we are dis-countenanced.

Countenance is what we humans crave more than anything else.

And what we dread more than anything else is ridicule. Being revealed for what we are: nothing, or next to nothing. Mortal mammals.

Countenance is a tenuous thing indeed, as Charlie Chaplin well knew. A mere banana peel suffices to destroy it.

Strolling down my street one afternoon, I passed a group of nine- or ten-year-old boys. Suddenly one of them broke away from the group and planted himself in my path with a threatening gesture. Startled, I drew up short and my features contracted in a grimace of alarm. End of story: the child went back to his friends, one hand raised in the V of victory. "See that? Not bad, eh? Not bad!" Yes, he had won: in the space of a single second, he had managed to ruffle my poise, interrupt my stroll, shake up my self-confidence, damage my dignity.

Without witnesses, he would never have done such a thing.

All narratives need a public.

The contemporary London fad known as "happy slapping" – young people filming each other as they kick or punch a perfect stranger on a subway platform, then posting the films on the Internet – has the same structure as the incident in my street, only slightly enlarged.

War has the same structure, greatly enlarged.

The goal of war, for each side, is to discountenance the enemy, wreak havoc with the foundations of his identity, and make sure it all gets publicized.

* * *

In deportation, slavery, and genocide, victims are first robbed of their stories.

Nothing could be more destabilizing, more anxiety-provoking, more panic-inducing, than to see the various elements of your identity knocked down like so many bowling pins.

Your house, your city, your profession, your clothes, your hair, your eyeglasses – gone.
Your name replaced by a number.
Families separated, languages mixed together ...
In these conditions, it is virtually impossible to hold your *self* together.
Before you die, you are already dead to your self.

You say you were a rabbi? A professor? A mother? A great actor? You are none of these things anymore – just look at you. You are ridiculous, that's what you are. A naked worm, a thing at my mercy, a doll. ... And in the end, literally a thing. A pile of bloody flesh. Dust. Ashes. And I – a hero. And my country – victorious.

* * *

All the world's a stage. And all of us are players, decked out with more or less convincing props.

In war, each side seeks to destroy the other's props.

What do you own that could never be wrested away from you?

My spiritual strength, you might answer. May it stand you in good stead.

However, if you think about how you acquired that spiritual strength, you will see that it came to you through fictions – that is, through the religious, political, or intimate fables with which you were inculcated, and to which you decided to adhere. Let's just hope that your fictions are rich, not poor.

Jean Améry bitterly observed that people who believed in God or the Revolution fared much better in the German concentration camps than disillusioned atheists like himself.

Thanks to the illusions they convey and the hope they engender, said Améry, political and religious fictions contribute more effectively to survival than all the philosophies that purport to debunk them.

Romain Gary knew this. His novels show the incredible moral strength derived by Polish Resistance fighters from the imaginary hero Nadejda (*A European Education*), or by prisoners in a German camp from the image of elephants stampeding across the savannah (*The Roots of Heaven*).

Personally, what keeps me going are love fables. Were I subjected to torture, however, I doubt that they'd hold out for more than a few hours (maybe only a few minutes – who knows?). Having little or no taste for heroism, I am clearly not cut out for extreme situations.

Fantasies are precious, miraculous things. They enable us to hang on in the face of adversity, our gaze unswervingly fixed on our ideal.

Fantasies are dangerous, terrifying things. They enable us to turn on the gas and exterminate our fellow creatures, our gaze unswervingly fixed on our ideal.

In both cases, the strength we derive from fictions is due to the presence of other people within ourselves. It comes from the texts and Ur-texts we have absorbed – first in our family circle, then at school, church, university, on television, and at the movies. ... All of these texts, through the process of *identification*, have shaped our *identities*.

Etty Hillesum was a voracious reader. She devoured books of psychology, poetry, Jewish and Christian mysticism. These rich fictions made her capable of identifying with the entire human race. Refusing to hate her enemy, she was radiant with happiness when she went to her death at Auschwitz.

Rudolf Hœss, who consumed a very limited number of texts, all of them simplistic and stereotyped, identified only with the *Führer's* values – obedience, hierarchy, the Aryan race, the German people. These bad fictions made him capable of running the gas chambers at Auschwitz with almost no twinges of conscience. Before being executed by the Poles in Nuremberg, he had the time to assess his experience and express, in his memoirs, at least a modicum of remorse.

Rare are those as wise as the elderly Japanese man who, after having fought in the Second World War, spent a decade in Siberia as a prisoner of the Russians. When asked if he had been brainwashed during captivity, he answered, "Yes, thank goodness! My brain definitely needed washing, after all the ideas of purity, hardness, and intransigence that had been pumped into it during my youth!"

* * *

When a collectivity is weakened, humiliated, or under threat, its members tend to listen to, believe, and obey their leaders in much the same way as children listen to, believe, and obey their parents.

This is why a majority of Americans bought George W. Bush's tall tale about Iraq being responsible for the 9/11 attacks.

In the Middle East, wars will continue to break out as long as the different peoples go on stubbornly clinging to their respective fictions. Naturally, the worse their situation gets, the more fiercely they tend to cling.

In Palestinian schools, children learn nothing about the Holocaust; thus, they find the massive arrival of Jews in Palestine, and the creation of the State of Israel in 1948, incomprehensible and shocking.

Israeli schoolchildren are taught little or nothing about the *Naqba* (or "Catastrophe"), in the course of which seven hundred thousand Palestinians were forced out of their homes, dispersed, exiled, or killed to make room for the new arrivals, the new country. This makes Arab resentment towards them indecipherable, not to say monstrous.

Though it is tempting to see the two situations as symmetrical (for symmetry is yet another fiction our brains find satisfying), they are not.

All we need to do is compare Israeli and Palestinian statistics in a few areas – not only average annual incomes and military budgets but education of women, percentage of children attending school, and especially *access to the novels and films of other cultures* – and then ask ourselves which of the two populations is more liable, in its religious and political speeches (assuming there is any distinction between the two) to preach hatred.

In France, one could do the same sort of statistics for young people who live in the culturally deprived suburbs and those who live in the city centres, then ask ourselves which of the two groups is more liable to think, speak, and act in oversimplistic ways. (Thus, the question asked by an angry Parisian intellectual, "Why do the immigrants' children slit the throat of the French language?" is worse than naïve; it is inept.)

The more a group is oppressed, compressed, and crushed, the more liable it is to subscribe to the Ur-text, painting reality in black and white and recommending violence to eliminate the black and impose the white.

When people are maintained, year after year, in a world of constraintand humiliation, they can hardly be expected to bring warm smiles and subtle arguments to the negotiation table. Endlessly reinforcing the security contingents around the "agitators" only makes them more and more primitive – and thus more and more dangerous.

* * *

When we go to war, staking out our territory, extending it, and appropriating other territories for more power and existence, our us bolsters itself with respect to the various *thems*.

Provided that, thanks to the texts and Ur-texts we have absorbed, the *thems* have first been interiorized as inferior or subhuman, war will create no moral problem for us whatsoever.

This reasoning was challenged by Jesus and by the philosophers of the Enlightenment, who postulated the equal value of all human lives. That did not put an end to it, however.

In the name of Jesus, in the name of the Enlightenment – more massacres.

It is likely that nothing will ever put an end to it, because whenever people's survival is at stake, their brains tend irresistibly to revert to the primitive narrative, the Ur-Text.

VIII

INTIMATE FABLES

"A great love is what happens when two dreams meet up, see eye to eye, and manage to escape reality to the end. So you see these wonderful couples living side by side, constantly inventing one another, and remaining faithful to their work of art despite all the traps of The Way Things Are ..."
— Romain Gary

Some fictions are violent; they lead to death.

Others are rich and beautiful; they lead to love.

We are human because — endlessly, indefatigably — we think, dream, talk, and tell ourselves stories about love and hatred.

Thus, love exists just as truly as hatred does – because imagination truly exists.

To love and be loved transforms us. It improves us, and it can also improve our performance.

From this point of view, it makes little difference whether we love God or a fellow human.

The French tennis player's girlfriend gives him a soulful look at the decisive moment in the match – and he wins. The Brazilian tennis player furtively touches the gold cross at his neck – and he wins.

Love has carried the day.

In all of its forms, love is a tale people tell themselves to make life livable.

Here again, to call it a tale implies neither that it does not really exist (tales really exist), nor that it is a lie (since we believe in it).

Like so many other human fictions, love is a source of narratives that *become* our reality.

I am not denying that your dog loves you; I am denying it thinks *I love you*. It disposes of neither an *I* nor a *you*, and thus cannot conceive of love.

Babies cannot conceive of love, either. The human child is a puppy (or a chimp) in the process of transcending itself through fiction.

In love as in war, myths and realities are perfectly inextricable.

Friendship
In human friendship, *I love you* means: I want our stories to become interwoven.

To love someone is to recognize, value, and *activate* their stories.

It is marvellous to see a person relax and blossom under the effect of your interest – the way a flower gradually unfolds, opens up, and reveals its colours to the sunlight.

Passionate Love
I magically and instantaneously endow you with every quality I cherish. I burn with desire for you – that magical other who will turn me, too, into what I have always longed to be.

The you can be a member of the opposite sex, or of my own.

To fall madly in love with someone is to find oneself suddenly vulnerable to their charm.

As the word *charm* suggests, seduction among human beings always involves magic, that is, imagination. You talk to me, you charm me, your words act upon me like a charm, they *are* a charm, casting a spell upon me and eliciting my own words in return. I charm, bewitch, and transport you, wafting you elsewhere.

Such extraordinary tales people tell themselves, when they make love lovingly!

Love-making is a *story* that can be more or less interesting. Routine copulation is as monotonous and predictable as a cheap novel, but when you are madly in love ... oh! First the preliminaries, the foreplay, then the thickening plot, the rising tension ... inventions, improvisations, confidences, exchanges, unexpected twists and turns ... and at last – always unique – the climax (a not-for-nothing-ambiguous term), followed by the dénouement (last caresses, murmurs, and then sleep) ...

I love X, X loves me: how many examinations did I pass

with flying colours as an adolescent, how many pages have I written as an adult, entranced by the magic of those phrases? Always the same words – whereas the identity of X changed constantly ...

The magic is *efficacious*. What matter that it is also *ephemeral?*

Yes: as Roland Barthes showed in his *Fragments of a Lover's Discourse*, disillusionments and disappointments invariably ensue. Not, as is commonly supposed, because the lovers' images cannot survive the confrontation with reality, but because the fictions of one cannot survive the confrontation with the fictions of the other.

When I am passionately in love with you, I dream and think about you constantly, carry you with me in my heart wherever I go. ... In so doing, I indulge quite literally in make-believe. I *make* myself *believe* that you are the most extraordinary person on earth.

It all comes from the imagination. Chimpanzees do not whisper sweet nothings into each other's ears.

What we love is an image, a representation of the other person. How could we possibly carry a flesh-and-blood person around inside our hearts?

All of us embark on our love stories with our minds teeming with fictions, from Heloise and Abelard to Romeo and Juliet, from *The Scarlet Letter* to the *Baghavad Gita*. There are no real people in our brains, only characters. Here as with war fables, our minds are constantly mingling historical celebrities with the heroes of novels or films ...

(*Mise en abyme*: an adulterous woman today fantasizes about Madame Bovary, who fantasized about the heroines of popular novels, who themselves fantasized about sentimental poetry ...)

Our ways of loving are inseparable from the tales of love that our culture makes available to us. (To convince ourselves of this we need only watch *Three Times*, that remarkable movie by Chinese director Hou Hsiao Hsien.)

When censorship prevents the circulation of texts about certain forms of love (courtly, erotic, mad ...), people are also deprived of the possibility of experiencing those forms.

In our parts of the world, where a premium is placed on individual destiny, two factors have radically transformed human sexual behaviour over the past couple of centuries: the advent of the novel and birth control.

These two factors have gradually led people to dissociate sexuality and reproduction. For the better (a more joyful approach to eroticism, for both men and women) and for the worse (a spectacular increase in pornography and prostitution).

Living Together

If I set up housekeeping with someone (whether because we are smitten with one another or because our parents reached an agreement), another type of love can grow up between us.

Rather than: "I tell myself his story in such a way as to make him absolutely desirable to me," it will be: "I have learned the basics of his story and he of mine; more importantly, over the days and years, we are writing a story together." This story can be beautiful or ugly; most often, it is a mixture of the two. But it is our story – that is, our life.

Experience creates essence.

Increasingly, in the modern Western world, people are free to invent their love stories as they see fit. They can add new characters (children, whether biological or adopted) or decide not to (contraception and abortion); they can thicken the plot (quarrels, betrayals, etc.); they can end one story (divorce) and begin another (remarriage). ... We all tell ourselves our love stories in such a way as to lend them maximum coherence and intensity.

All this, as well, hinges on our gift for fabulation.

Parental Love
There is nothing instinctive about parental love.

What is instinctive is to do everything in our power to ensure that our babies will survive (us) – including, as Elisabeth Badinter has shown, farming them out to country nurses if they can take better care of them than we.

For human beings, however, having babies cannot be reduced to the reproductive instinct. Because we live in narrativity, our children fictionally connect us – both to the past (we care about passing on to them those elements of our inheritance we see as precious) and to the future (we invest them with our hopes for success and happiness).

Even for this, love is not indispensable. In some parts of the world, parents treat their children harshly, subject them to stringent discipline, inflict violent punishment on them and exploit their working power.

But love, but love. How does it arise, when indeed it does arise, in the parent-child relationship?

It has nothing to do with genes, though genetics are often invoked to justify and reinforce it. In the love between parent and child, the *idea* of blood can play a crucial role, but blood plays no role whatsoever.

A human baby will bond with its mother, or with any other person who gives it motherly care. That bonding, however, is not yet love.

Love requires a lengthy, complex process of initiation. It is conveyed by narratives and is indissociable from them.

A human mother, being by definition an adult and thus immersed in fictions, bonds with her child (or any child declared to be hers) by telling herself "this child is mine."

I have seen women friends, both French and Canadian, receive a photo of the child they were planning to adopt, currently still living at the far ends of the earth, and cry out at once, "Isn't he beautiful? Isn't she adorable?" Though they had not yet set eyes on the child, they focalized their maternal passion on it in just the same way as biological mothers do. They memorized all the details of its history, crowed in delight at its every feature. ... If they later learned that child in question was too ill to be adopted or had been given to another couple, they experienced it as a personal tragedy – whereas, of course, thousands of unknown children died every day without their batting an eyelash.

Whether or not a baby shares our chromosomes, the fact of telling ourselves "This is my son" or "This is my daughter" gives it incommensurable value. Children inject massive doses of Meaning into our life stories. *That* is why we love them.

* * *

The fiction of parental love is crucial to the survival of the human species, for a reason which is still little known: *human babies are born several months premature.*

Were they carried to term, given the large circumference of their skulls (due to *Homo sapiens'* oversized brain) and the narrowness of their mother's pelvises (due to the vertical position adopted by *Homo sapiens*), all deliveries would be fatal – to the mother, to the baby, or to both.

That would not do at all. In the space of a few decades, humanity would be wiped out.

Thus, human babies are born prematurely and need to be helped, protected, and educated for years before they can manage on their own. It takes them six months just to sit up by themselves! Whereas baby gorillas learn to walk in a matter of days, baby humans require a whole year. ... As for fending for themselves foodwise, they only manage this after ... seven or eight years in poor countries, fifteen or sixteen elsewhere ... and in the opulent Western world, a good two decades or more!

This means that human females need to take care of their little ones far longer and more intensively than chimp females.

It is quite possible that human language was born in the course of these exceptionally lengthy and intense exchanges between mothers and their children.

And, along with language, misogyny ...

Marriage
As motherhood demanded so much time and effort of human females, they had to do their utmost to keep their males attached to them, and to their little ones. No easy task.

Whereas both motherhood and fatherhood are experienced as fictions, motherhood usually involves a palpable physiological reality (gestation, delivery, lactation, etc). Fatherhood, on the other hand, *seems* fictional.

In a tale-telling species (the only one to grasp the connection between sexuality and reproduction), it is rather wounding for one sex to have to admit that it owes its existence to the other, that females give birth to both males and females, and that males play an apparently minor role in the crucial affair of reproduction.

Whence men's need to proclaim their fatherhood loudly and insistently – through the virginity taboo, the punishment of female adultery, the transmission of the patronym, and so forth. Whence, as well, in male-female relations, the most widespread fiction of all: that the woman "belongs" to the man.

He "possesses" her, both in the short-term (copulation), and in the long-term (marriage).

Marriage is a human reality – that is, a fiction – to which our species decided to adhere several thousand years ago because it was conducive to our survival. When children are born, it helps us determine who their father is.

Neither chimpanzees nor bonobos care about who is who's father. Patrimony and patronyms leave them cold. True, they form couples; and true, they are sometimes unfaithful to their mates. Unlike us, however, they do not spin endless tales about paternity for the purpose of consolidating families, clans, tribes, nations, and civil societies.

The nuclear family is one of the great specificities of *Homo sapiens*. Instead of constantly competing for the favours of the same females, each human male could lay claim to absolute power over *one* woman; this enabled them to go off and work together with their minds at rest. The exceptional degree of collaboration among the males of our species is what gave rise to ... civilization!

In other words, the idea that each man was the exclusive owner of one woman, though belied on countless occasions, enabled humanity to make great leaps forward. We humans have now leapt so far forward that we have inflicted permanent damage on our planet and are capable of blowing ourselves up several times over.

The Oppression of Women
Though male chimpanzees are notoriously jealous, sexist, and possessive, only humans devise laws, rituals, and taboos to *codify* the relationships between males and females.

None of the other higher primate species ever forbade males to shake hands with females, or to approach them during their periods. None ever concealed the faces, heads, or whole bodies of females under veils. None ever forced females to stay locked up in their homes, or to hold their tongues in the presence of their sexual partners. Chimpanzees do not slice off the clitorises of young females to make sure they will get no pleasure from coitus, nor do they sew up their vaginas only to rip them open again with knives on their wedding nights, nor do they crush the bones of their feet to be able to squeeze them into tiny shoes, thus crippling them for life, nor do they write laws enumerating their specific rights and obligations, nor do they stone them to death if they have sex with more than one partner.

This being said, it would be absurd to describe men's oppression of women as the result of some universal plot. In our species, it is more like a second nature.

Probably since humanity's inception, women qua mothers have been excluded from certain sacred acts and rituals. The rationale was either that they were impure, and must not approach these domaines on pain of defiling them, or that they already had their own sacred domaine (childbirth), and needed no other.

In many ways, this is true: having children indubitably confers Meaning on women's lives. For most women, even today, motherhood is a self-evident and irrefutable reason to go on living – whereas men are perpetually compelled to devise, construct, display, lay claim to, insist upon, and invent Meaning for their lives as best they can.

This is why, traditionally, males have monopolized activities with high levels of Meaning: universities, religious hierarchies, literature, and war. Prestige guaranteed.

Women had no need of that prestige; therefore, they were barred from it.

Prostitution

Prostitution is an overdetermined phenomenon.

Firstly, defined as the exact opposite of mothers, prostitutes absorb men's rage, jealousy, and resentment vis-à-vis the mothers whose mercy they were at as little boys. Every little boy spends the first few years of his life in a state of utter dependence on a woman who controls, bullies, punishes, kisses, and caresses him – a woman who is his universe. As an adult, provided that he can pay, he has the right to take symbolic revenge upon her by controlling, bullying, punishing, or caressing an anonymous woman.

Secondly, given that human males insist on being the exclusive owners of their children's mothers, they tend to stipulate that The Mother *per se* is pure, virtuous, and asexual. Whence their need for The Whore to embody sexuality, impurity, and vice.

In non-tale-telling species, of course, females are neither clean nor dirty, neither virtuous nor corrupt.

"Mother" is a role. "Whore," even more so.

Depending on the society, a human female can be deemed a whore if she:
— leaves the house without putting on her veil
— speakes to a male who is not her husband
— dances, sings, smokes, or performs on a stage
— copulates with strangers for money ...

No one can be a whore. All that anyone can do is *play* the whore.

Even professional prostitutes only play the whore. Day after day, they pronounce the same lines without adhering to them, privately convinced that, "deep down," they are not whores but mothers, or students, or impoverished young women, saving up money to feed their children, start a business, pay for their studies ... while still dreaming, perhaps, that their Prince Charming will come along someday ...

The fictive nature of prostitution by no means protects prostitutes from its real effects (contempt, hatred, ostracism, exploitation, physical violence, murder).

Real women die every day, simply for having taken on the role of whore in the great theatre of humanity.

Rape

The victim's lack of desire intensifies my own, and I impose it on her by force. In so doing, I spoil her intimate fables and those of her husband or lover.

The victim can be male or female, but is more usually female. Blithely ignoring her past, her specific life story, and her individual identity, I inflict my own interpretation on her. I decree that she is *nothing but* this thing which I despise and defile – in wartime, *nothing but a* Croatian, or a German, etc.; in peacetime, *nothing but* a woman (or a man treated like a woman). What defiles her is not my sperm but my will, which negates and obliterates her own. When I ejaculate in her body, I want the event to mean not the beginning of a new life but the end of *her* life: never again will she be able to tell herself beautiful love stories.

Certain animal species, including chimpanzees, practise rape – that is, males sometimes copulate with females against their will, to affirm their power in the face of their usual sexual partners. Only human rape, however, is imbued with Meaning: the act of love transformed into an act of hate; the construction of a lineage turned into its destruction.

Feminism
We human females of the Western world have come a long way.

First thousands of years of oppression, then ideologies of equality and human rights, and finally, freedoms won after centuries of struggle. We are now at a far remove from the first "casting" our species devised for itself.

Today, Western women can earn university diplomas, vote, change partners, and choose their baby's birthdate, sex, and name in advance, very much the way novelists do with their characters. Moreover, machines (and sometimes even husbands) help them with their housekeeping and maternal duties, making the latter more agreeable than ever before.

Today, in other words, every woman, like every man, theoretically has the right to compose the novel of her life as she sees fit.

As usual, though, there is a flip side to the coin. Our hardwon freedoms deprive us of our old, reassuring certainties as to the Meaning of our lives – often plunging us, like men, into anxiety and depression.

Moreover, these freedoms make us liable (also like men) to founder on the modern fiction *par excellence* – that of the utterly autonomous individual, the person who needs no bonds.

IX

PERSONAS AND PERSONS

"[Staring at the African masks in the Trocadero Museum], I suddenly understood what purpose sculpture had served for the Negroes. Why would they sculpt in this way rather than another? I mean, they were not cubists, after all! ... The fetishes all played the same role. They were weapons designed to help people stop obeying the spirits and become independent. They were tools. If we give a form to the spirits, we become independent."
– Pablo Picasso

Again: no matter how far back we go in time, or how deeply we plunge into desert or jungle, there is no record of a human tribe ever having been content to live in "reality," to register it and comment on it without telling stories about it.

If fictions with characters are ubiquitous in our species, it is because *we are the characters of our own lives* – and because, unlike chimpanzees, we need to learn our roles.

The root word of *person is persona*, an ancient term (the Romans having borrowed it from the Etruscans) meaning mask.

A human being is someone who wears a mask.

Every person is a character who plays a role.

What makes our species unique is that we spend our lives acting out our lives.

The roles offered us will be more or less diverse and flexible, depending on the society into which we are born. We shall be taught to play our roles convincingly, given models to imitate and narratives about them to commit to memory.

Identity is built up through identification. The self is made up of others.

Yes – all of us need what Samuel Beckett called *company*.

Even the brain of the most misanthropic, monastic, rationalist philosopher is literally crawling with the presence of other people.

Novelists often take pride in being free of the religious illusions which handicap the rest of humanity. ... Yet their minds are inhabited (not to say possessed) by their characters, just as the minds of superstitious peasants are possessed by Jesus-Mary-Joseph, or the minds of madmen by the devil.

* * *

Today as yesterday, one of the important ways in which we seek and find Meaning is by projecting ourselves imaginarily into other people. What then occurs is a crystallization, an essentialization – a "precipitation," as it were – of hitherto vague and impalpable affects.

Throughout human history, people have drawn moral lessons from characters as depicted in cultural fictions, whether mighty (religions) or modest (folks tales and fables). *And the moral of the story is ..."*

Identification engenders ethics.

The Ur-Text allows every human being, including the illiterate, to recognize him- or herself in a group. *They*, the bad guys, are threatening what We, the good guys, cherish most in the world (our freedom, our civilization, our faith, our women, our wealth, our territorial integrity, and so forth). Simple fictions.

The great cultural texts – sacred books, Bibles and Korans, myths and war epics – enable us to identify with the history of our people. Through slanted stories, beautiful poetry, and edifying parables, they teach readers lessons, give them a clear and unambiguous code of conduct, provide them with basic ethics. Simple fictions.

In Greek tragedy, the hero is torn between two forces of destiny, two sacred duties, or two gods. By identifying with his dilemmas, the audience undergoes catharsis, thus helping to purge society of its ills. Through the public performance of the conflicts to which it gives rise, the clear distinction between Good and Evil is reiterated ... and reinforced.

The protagonists of folk tales are less heroic. They are more like ourselves – that is, imperfect and contradictory. Their stories, however, remain simple and almost always edifying.

Modern novels, whose characters are ordinary people,

incite us to identify neither with perfection (invariably guilt-inducing) nor, negatively, with monstruosity (foils such as the Devil, the Witch, the Criminal) – but with ambiguity, doubt, and uncertainty.

The modern novel appeared in seventeenth-century Europe and came fully into its own in the eighteenth, when religious certainties had been undermined by science.

What science shows us is that behind facts, there are *causes*, not *reasons*. That changes everything.

The old values based on the traditional constraints of religion, clan, and family no longer seeming self-evident, Europeans needed to find or invent new ones.

Whence: love marriages instead of arranged marriages; literature and philosophy instead of religion.

The individual is the result of these transformations.

The advent of the modern novel is inseparable from that of the individual.

Increasingly aware of the arbitrary nature of their presence on Earth, but also of their freedom, European intellectuals began to feel responsible for their own destinies. This made them dizzy. Out of their dizziness arose Romanticism – in two complementary forms, one social (spawning revolutionaries), the other individual (spawning nihilists).

Science does not produce Meaning; rather, it produces correlations independent of ourselves. We remain fragile, and the world remains threatening. No scientific discovery can make us immortal, or even eliminate pain and conflict from our existence.

Though we no longer exclaim *It's the end of the world!* when we see an eclipse of the moon, the rational explanation of eclipses – or electrical storms, or illnesses – does not obviate our need to seek and find Meaning in life.

Even today, of course, the great religious narratives continue to fulfill this function. In addition to those traditional conveyors of Meaning, however, the past two centuries have seen an unprecedented proliferation of secular narratives, which circulate in countless forms (literature, theatre, cinema, television, video games, the Internet ...).

Thus, in the modern world (which is not the entire world), every individual's brain has its own associations, its own combination of fictions, its own unique way of keeping itself company.

* * *

Novelists often elicit skepticism when they claim that their characters are as "real" to them as flesh-and-blood human beings.

Yet this should not be surprising – given that, in our brains, *living people are characters.*

Think of all the people who surround you – some of them loved ones, others mere acquaintances, still others strangers – all your relatives, friends and neighbours, your country's politicians, your neighbourhood storekeepers, famous movie actors, anonymous crowds seen on television. ... To these, add the people whom you have *never* seen but who you know to exist or to have existed: farmers in Zimbabwe, workers in Russian nuclear plants, your best friend's brother (the one who lives in Buenos Aires), sixteenth-century writers, Alexander the Great, the millions of Italians killed by the plague in 1348. ... What you carry around in your brain is a more or less detailed *image* of all these people – an image which, spontaneously and automatically, you revise, retouch, and readapt every time you see or think about them. By definition, all of these images are incomplete, and yet they seem "complete" to you at any given moment.

Novelists capitalize on this automatic "filling-out" process when they sketch out a character at the beginning of a book. Their words spark off memories, associations, flashes of recognition in their readers' brains – and if they are gifted, the spell takes effect: within a few pages, the readers start living with their characters as if they knew them personally.

Exactly what happens when we take a character's story into our hearts and make it our own? How, in other words, does novelistic identification work? Can and does it suggest a possible ethics for life in society?

* * *

Some contemporary thinkers are firmly convinced that the novel is the supreme art form for the expression and exploration of the individual.

The protagonists they admire are defined essentially negatively – that is, by what they (fortunately) lack. They have no debts or responsibilities towards other people. No children and, ideally (like Roquentin in Sartre's *Nausea*), no parents, either. No nationality, no party, no uterus (that goes without saying) – in short, no determinism of any kind. These thinkers see the individual as the foundation, centre, and meaning of everything – pure freedom, with the novel as his kingdom.

This is a narrow definition indeed of the novelistic genre, and one that matches only a very small number of books. Countless novels, the world over, give us a more complete and complex picture of humanity.

That the advent of the novel is inseparable from that of the individual by no means implies that novels are intrinsically individualistic. Whether we like it or not, there is no such thing as freedom without ties, for the simple reason that without ties there can be nothing – neither language nor humanity nor individuals, still less *free* individuals.

People do not learn to speak all by themselves. Language is neither more nor less than the presence of others within us. Without that presence, we should have no access to the human world.

"Total freedom" does not bring forth individuals. A person who *truly* had no family, offspring, tribe, or nation would not be an individual, to say nothing of a writer; he would be an *enfant sauvage*.

Mute, mad, or both.

Modern individuals experience a permanent tension between the longing for freedom and the need for ties. This tension, and the countless stories to which it gives rise, is the territory of the novel.

* * *

In *Diary of a Bad Year*, South African author J.M. Coetzee (now settled in Australia) shows an elderly writer summing up his life and work in a rather negative way.

"Scenes of mass celebration," he writes after watching a cricket match on television, give me a glimpse of what I have missed out on in life, what I excluded myself from by persisting in being the kind of creature I am: the joy of belonging to (belonging in) a mass, of being swept along on currents of mass feeling. What a realization for someone to come to who was born in Africa, where the mass is the norm and the solitary the aberration! As a young man, I never for a moment allowed myself to doubt that only from a self disengaged from the mass and critical of the mass could true art emerge."

In order to practise their art, novelists need to be both intimately acquainted with the outside world and cut off from it. No one will ever resolve this contradiction – and fortunately so, for were it to be resolved, the novel would vanish.

"Whatever art has come from my hand," Coetzee's character goes on, "has in one way or another expressed and even gloried in this disengagement. But what sort of art has that been, in the end? Art that is not great-souled, as the Russians would say, that lacks generosity, fails to celebrate life, lacks love."

Many European novels today, bent on proclaiming human solitude and deploring human mortality, are similarly lacking in greatness of soul.

* * *

Mister Pip, a novel by New Zealander Lloyd Jones, shows us how novelistic fictions can be a source of ethics and help us to live our lives.

It is the tale of a group of aboriginal children on an island off the coast of New Zealand, during a time of political strife. The village is under threat of attack, and daily life is in such a state of upheaval that the schools have been closed down.

One day, the only remaining white man in the village, a certain Mr. Watts (nicknamed "Pop Eye" because of his bulging eyeballs) reopens the school in the middle of the jungle and starts reading out loud to the dumbfounded children. The book from which he reads is *Great Expectations* by Charles Dickens.

As of the first day, he makes the great British novelist accessible to his pupils by comparing his work to what constitutes the first fiction in all our lives, that is, our given names. "No one in the history of your short lives," he tells them, "has used the same voice as you with which to say your name. This is yours. Your special gift that no one can ever take from you. This is what our friend and colleague Mr. Dickens used to construct his stories with."

Matilda, the novel's young narrator (aged thirteen), soon becomes obsessed with Dickens's hero, Pip. This upsets her mother, Dolores, who fears that all these "false" stories will cast doubt upon the "truths" with which she has been inculcating her daughter ever since she was born. Dolores's truths are basically two in number: the family tree and the Gospels.

"At night my mum maintained a restless silence. ... She asked if us kids ever heard the word of the Good Lord from Pop Eye. 'Mr Watts does not use the Bible,' I said. She let that sit in the air, as if it were a betrayal of our very safety. Then she returned to her other preoccupation, testing me with the names of relatives and fish and birds from our family tree. I failed miserably. I could think of no reason to remember them, whereas I knew the name of every character I had met in *Great Expectations* because I had heard them speak. They had shared their thoughts with me, and sometimes as Mr Watts read aloud I could even see their faces. Pip, Miss Havisham and Joe Gargery were more part of my life than my dead relatives, even the people around me."

Before long, little Matilda starts wondering, "Where's the value in knowing a few scattered and unreliable facts about dead relatives when you could know all there was to know about a made-up person such as Pip?"

That is indeed the central question raised by Jones's remarkable novel: what are the similarities and differences among the various fictive beings who inhabit us – our ancestors, the characters of religious stories, and the protagonists of novels?

Matilda's mother is adamant: religion must win out over literature. "That night she asked me if I believed in the devil. Stupidly I answered, No. She asked me why – after everything I had been told about the devil – so I recited Mr Watts' words back to her, I said the devil was a symbol. He is not living flesh. 'Nor is Pip,' she said. But I had my answer ready. 'You cannot hear the devil's voice. You can hear Pip's.'"

Furious, Dolores goes to school with her daughter the next day and confronts her professor. "'My daughter, my lovely Matilda,' she began, 'tells me she does not believe in the devil. She believes in Pip.' ... 'Well, Dolores,' he said calmly, 'what if we were to say that on the page Pip and the devil have the same status?'"

At home again, Dolores makes fun of the professor, trying to devalue him in her daughter's eyes: "'Why do you look to an ignorant, dangerous man for a teacher? This is how crazy the world has become. Can your Mr Watts build a house? Can he paddle out to the reef at sunset and sneak up on a shoal of parrot fish? Your Mr Watts is dependent on other souls to feed him and his wife. He is nothing by himself.'"

"'Once upon a time,' Matilda says, 'I would have walked away from her attack on Mr. Watts – now I listened. In her mocking I could hear Estella.'"

At that precise moment, when she *decides to go on listening to her mother* because she reminds her of a character from Dickens, Matilda shows that she has mastered the art of the novel.

Yes: characters in novels, like characters in religious stories but in far more complex ways, give us models and anti-models for behaviour. They afford us precious distance from the people around us, and (even more importantly) from ourselves. They help us see that our lives are fictions, and that, therefore, we have the power to act upon them and change their course.

Why is Pip so important to Matilda? Because, like Coetzee's aging writer in his youth, Matilda lives in a world in which the I finds it hard to exist, being constantly silenced and subsumed by the *we*. Pip is the first genuine individual of her acquaintance, the first person she sees taking his life in hand and making his own decisions about the path he wants to follow.

She asks Mr. Watts why Dickens's young hero changes his name. Here is what her teacher answers: "'Pip is an orphan. He is like an emigrant. He is in the process of migrating from one level of society to another. A change of name is as good as a change of clothes. It is to help him on his way. It is hard to be a perfect human being, Matilda,' he said. 'Pip is only human. He has been given the opportunity to turn himself into whomever he chooses. He is free to choose. He is even free to make bad choices.'"

Years later, after having left her native island, attended university in Brisbane, and written a thesis on Charles Dickens, Matilda gets in touch with Mr. Watts's first wife, listens to her tale, and learns many unexpected facts about the teacher she so admired and thought she knew.

"I suppose it is possible to be all of these things," she says to herself. "To sort of fall out of who you are into another, as well as to journey back to some essential sense of self. We only see what we see. I have no idea of the man June Watts knew. I only know the man who took us kids by the hand and taught us how to re-imagine the world, and to see the possibility of change, to welcome it into our lives. Your ship could come in any time, and that ship could take many forms."

That is an admirable summary of what novels can do.

Instead of saying, like traditional stories, *This is the way the world is, was, and always has been*, they say, *We only see what we see.*

In so saying, they teach us – the phrase is rich enough to warrant repetition – *to re-imagine the world, and to see the possibility of change, to welcome it into our lives.*

* * *

To sum up: there is no impermeable border between "real life" and fiction; each feeds – and feeds off – the other.

We can act and comprehend only through identification, projection, introjection, simplification, essentialization, resemblance, and representation – in a word, through masks.

The *persona* is, quite simply, the human way of being in the world.

X

WHY THE NOVEL

"They hurled the books to the floor, trampling them and tearing them up in front of my eyes. ... And I told them not to tear them up, for a multitude of books is never dangerous, but a single book is dangerous; and I told them not to tear them up for reading many books leads to wisdom and reading only one leads to ignorance armed with madness and hatred."
– Danielo Kis

Novels are written, and can only be written, where survival is guaranteed. Whenever their survival is at stake, human beings will tend to adhere unreservedly to the fictions which underlie and reinforce their identities.

Those countries which allow people to revise the fictions of their given identities – by changing religions, political parties, opinions, or even sexes – are also those in which novels are written and read.

To enter literature is to abandon the Ur-Text. To go beyond primitive narratives.

To be primitive is to stick to one's identity as if it were a fixed, unchanging essence, and to identify only with people like oneself.

Hitler's Germany and Stalin's Russia were primitive countries. They forced their peoples to adhere to the Ur-Text, burning or banishing stories that deviated too much from it.

In many ways, early twenty-first-century America has been behaving like a primitive country.

Fortunately, there are many excellent novelists in the United States.

Unfortunately, fewer than one American out of two reads more than one novel per year.

Non-readers are potentially dangerous, as they will tend to have a preference for simplistic narratives and can be easily manipulated by churches, governments, and the media.

The novel, both in its historical emergence and in its everyday consumption, is inseparable from the individual. It is intrinsically *civilizing*.

(An aside: it is possible that women, at least in the Western world, are more civilized than men – not only because women read far more novels than men do, but because, from childhood onward, reading accustoms them to seeing the world [including themselves] through the eyes of others [men]!)

Reading novels – and, through them, learning to identify with the *characters* of another time, social milieu, or culture – gives us distance from our own, received identies. This can help us to decipher other cultures, and gradually learn to identify with the people who belong to them.

A country's voluntary fictions (stories) provide better access to its reality than its involuntary fictions (History).

Terrorism being neither more nor less than the result of bad fictions, what our governments should do is not manufacture more weapons but rather, in the countries where it has taken root, favour, encourage, and promote the translation, publication, and distribution of the masterpieces of world literature.

Nothing could be more useful, or more important.

The more people think of themselves as realistic, the more they tend to dismiss novels as being superfluous, silly, or a waste of time, the more liable they are to slide towards the Ur-Text – that is, towards vehemence, violence, criminality, the oppression of their loved ones, or of women, or of those whom they consider to be weak, or of an entire people.

This applies as much to the owners of big companies, multibillionaire arms salesmen, and ambitious politicians as it does to inner-city kids involved in gang warfare or Islamist fanatics plotting feverishly in European capitals.

All of these individuals have one important trait in common – they are too busy to read.

* * *

In the ideal City imagined by Plato, only the Guardians were to have access to the truth. To behave reasonably, the philosopher believed, the masses needed to be told fibs – for instance, that human beings were naturally divided into groups (Gold, Silver, and Bronze) with different destinies.

My own conviction is just the opposite: namely, that the elite should renounce its monopoly on good fictions and make it its duty to share and disseminate them as widely as possible.

Concretely, this means that schools should no longer be content with ensuring that children acquire their country's literary "canon," while simultaneously aggrandizing it with patriotism and anesthetizing it with theory.

What children need to acquire is the love of reading *per se*: the desire – and the ability – to devour literature from all over the world.

If they do not see what good reading does us, they will not find it interesting; thus, it is essential that we know what good it does us.

* * *

True, bad novels exist! Many novels are racist, nationalist, Manichean, sentimental, boring, pretentious, useless, or silly ...

True, even excellent novels can be badly read – rumour has it that John Lennon's assassin gleaned the order to commit his crime from J.D. Salinger's *Catcher in the Rye* ...

True, a great novelist can turn into a despicable, racist, murder-loving individual (Céline) ...

True, even people who have read hundreds of novels can be led, under extreme circumstances, to kill their own children or recommend the use of torture ...

True, whenever a group feels threatened, it will tend to revert to its primitive, gregarious reflexes and recite the Ur-Text. This is what happened to the American media, even the most noble among them, in the wake of 9/11.

Nonetheless, the characteristics of the novel – the way in which it explores the tension between individual and society, between freedom and determinism, and encourages us to identify with people unlike ourselves – make it capable of playing a role in ethics.

* * *

Over the past couple of decades, our societies have shown a growing mistrust vis-à-vis "fiction." Many people no longer want to be "taken in." Conveniently forgetting all of the fictions they swallow without knowing it, and which are an integral part of their identities, they now demand that everything they read and see on television be "true."

Whence, in contemporary literature, the popularity of the genre known as "autofiction." Those writers who continue to think of themselves as novelists, and of their books as novels, are told to "'fess up': Come on, now, this character here is basically yourself, isn't it? And this other one is your father? All this is a thinly disguised transposition of your own life story."

What readers should strive to recognize in the characters of a novel, of course, is not the author but themselves.

In the world of images, the same trend has given rise to "reality shows." Here, living human beings are used as "characters." They act out reassuringly simplistic fictions, in which spectators can effortlessly recognize the most rudimentary psychological postures of our species – jealousy, cupidity, disappointment, pride, anger, humiliation ...

This is a distressing sign of impoverishment ... whereas art's mission is not to impoverish but to enrich – not to slavishly transcribe the raw material of human existence but, refracting it through one or several particular minds, to help us to understand it.

* * *

The prisoner's question which inspired me to write the present book – "What's the point of making up stories when reality is so incredible?" – implied that the goal of literature is to surprise, impress, or dazzle us – in other words, to boggle our minds.

Only bad literature sets itself that goal.

As a rule, novelists do not set out to create a world more astonishing or incredible than reality.

Nothing can beat human reality. It is insuperable –for its madness and its ingeniosity, its cruelty and its grace.

What the novel *can* do, on the other hand, is to give us *another point of view* on reality. To enable us to step back from it, analyze it, see how it has been slapped together, criticize its underlying myths.

When you read a contemporary short story out loud to a group of prisoners, then discuss it with them, they often express surprise at two things: firstly, that it is possible to spend two hours passionately analyzing the motivations of people who do not exist, and secondly, that the *dénouement*, instead of feeling like an ending, often leaves the reader up in the air. In other words, the story's Meaning, much like the Meaning of life, must be deduced not from how it winds up but from how it unfolds.

What were the fictions that gave rise to the "incredible realities" of the women locked up at Fleury-Mérogis? Of what human follies had they been the subject or the object?

Love fables (jealousies, marital quarrels leading to murder), fables of motherly perfection (leading to infanticide), political or religious fables (making them willing or even eager to set bombs), fables about money or drugs leading to happiness ...

Here, then, is what I came up with as a tentative response to the prisoner's cry from the heart: "*Just* because *human reality is shot through and through with simplistic, involuntary fictions, it is important to invent complex, voluntary ones ...*"

Instead of presenting itself as truth, like the millions of other fictions which surround, invade, and define us, literature lays its cards on the table. *I am a fiction*, it tells us. Love me for what I am. Use me to feel your freedom, push back your limits, discover and awaken your own creativity. Follow the twists and turns of my characters and make them your own; allow them to enlarge your universe. Dream me, dream with me, never forget to dream.

Putting our feet in the author's footsteps, we learn to hear the unique *musique* of his or her language – and gradually, if the magic takes effect, our mind leaves the ground and starts to soar, eventually *partaking* in the divine prerogative of creation. Yes, through literature, we can sense that element of divinity hidden within each and all of us (and nowhere else!). Through it, in secret, in silence, ephemerally but truly, we become gods.

Not only that, but – at least temporarily – we become better people! Yes, every good novel is also an appeal on behalf of ethics, but of a very special kind.

Unlike our religious, familial, and political fictions, literary fiction does not tell us what is good and what is bad. Its ethical mission is to show us the truth of human beings – a truth which is always mixed, impure, filled with ironies, doubts, and abysses. (The minute a novelist starts imposing her vision of good upon us, she betrays her vocation and damages her book.)

Whereas our lives in society incite us to pronounce cut-and-dried judgments, taking sides only with the people we resemble and condone, the novel ushers us into a more variegated moral universe. The diametrical opposite of the Ur-Text, it helps us hear the true music of the world, which is neither the harmony of heaven nor infernal cacophony.

Absorbed in a novel, we are in fact far more moral than when we act as citizens, parents, spouses, or church members. Since all the events unfold within the privacy of our brains, and we do not feel threatened by those verbal beings known as characters, we often listen to them with more tolerance, more curiosity, and more benevolence than the flesh-and-blood people who surround us. Not only do we forgive them their weaknesses, we are actually *grateful* for them!

When we encounter "evil" people in a novel (criminals, religious fanatics, castrating bitches, violent parents, etc.), our impulse is less to condemn than to comprehend them – to let their stories develop in our minds and try to see, if not how we might resemble them, at least how they got that way.

By presenting itself as a fiction, by allowing us to *choose* it, literature temporarily frees us from the obligations and constraints of the countless fictions to which we are *subjected*. It makes us the gift of a reality which, though recognizable, is more precise, more profound, more intense, fuller, and longer-lasting than the reality of the outside world. Ideally, it can give us the strength to go back to that reality and decipher it, too, with greater subtlety.

It can even lead us – such things have been seen – to act upon it.

* * *

How many times have we heard the old refrain: "Look, Mao recited reams of classic Chinese poetry! Stalin loved classical music! The Nazis thrilled to poetry and opera on the weekend and committed mass murder the rest of the week!"

All of these things are true, and admittedly upsetting. A novel, however, is neither an opera nor a poem. Poetry is read in solitude, but it does not tell stories; rather, it evokes *moments*, particular *states* of the mind, the soul, the world. Opera, though it tells stories, is experienced collectively, both on stage and in the audience. Like the cinema, it encourages shared emotion, often enhanced by music.

Only the novel combines the two crucial factors of *narration* and *solitude*. It espouses the narrativity of every human existence, but – for author and reader alike – requires silence and solitude, and allows interruption, meditation, rereading.

Plays and films can also incite us to identify with people unlike ourselves, to combat Manicheism through nuance, and to replace the ethics of identity with an ethics of identification. Only the novel demands the active contribution of individual thought, since its action unfolds entirely in that most intimate of all places – the human brain. Moreover, it allows us to enter the brains of others and (as with Matilda and Mister Pip) become intimate witnesses to all their thoughts and doubts, fears and contradictions, memories and hopes ...

Narrative empathy is the basis for equality and exchange between the prisoner and myself. Alone of all the arts, literature allows us to *explore other people's inner existence.*

That is its sovereign privilege, and its value. Inestimable. Irreplaceable.

* * *

It is neither feasible nor desirable to banish fictions from human existence. They are vital to us – indeed, they are our very substance. They create our reality, and they help us endure it. They are reassuring, unifying, endlessly useful. We have seen that they give rise to both the best and the worst in human behaviour – to both genocide and Bach's *G-Minor Chaconne for Violin Solo*.

All we can try to do is choose rich, beautiful, complex, nuanced fictions instead of simple, brutal ones.

Schopenhauer and all the contemporary European writers who, whether explicitly or implicitly, have adopted his nihilist philosophy – from Cioran to Bernhard and from Houellebecq to Jelinek – spent their childhood in the grips of a powerfully constraining fiction, either religious or political. Having later come to understand that Heaven, Hell, and the Radiant Future were balderdash, and that the Meaning of human life was determined neither by God nor by History, they came to the conclusion that it had none, that it was nothing but horror and grotesquerie; thus, they began ranting and raving against it.

Nothing could be more absurd.

Life has all sorts of Meanings – all the ones we give it.

That the human condition is fiction is no reason to spit upon it.

It is up to us to make it interesting.

SOURCES

Améry, J., *At the Mind's Limits: Contemplations by a Survivor on Auschwitz and Its Realities*. Bloomington, IN: Indiana University Press, 1984.

Anonymous, *A Woman in Berlin: Eight Weeks in the Conquered City: A Diary*. Trans. Philip Boehm. New York: Metropolitan Books, 2000.

Ashforth, A., *Witchcraft, Violence and Democracy in South Africa*. Chicago: University of Chicago Press, 2005.

Auffret, S., *Des couteaux contre des femmes*. Paris: Editions des femmes, 1983.

Blackmore, S., *The Meme Machine*. Oxford: Oxford University Press, 1999.

————, *Consciousness: A Very Short Introduction*. Oxford: Oxford University Press, 2005.

Bodei, R., *La sensation du déjà vu*. Paris: Seuil, 2007.

Carrière, J.-C., *Tous en scène*. Paris: Editions Odile Jacob, 2007.

Coetzee, J.M., *Diary of a Bad Year*. Melbourne: Text Publishers, 2007.

Damasio, A.R., *The Feeling of What Happens: Body and Emotion in the Making of Consciousness*. New York: Harcourt, 2000.

———, *Looking for Spinoza: Joy, Sorrow and the Feeling Brain*. New York: Harcourt, 2003.

Dennett, D.C., *Consciousness Explained*. New York: Penguin Books, 1993.

Diamond, J., *The Rise and Fall of the Third Chimpanzee*. London: Vintage, 2002.

Flahault, F., "Récits de fiction et représentations partagées," *L'Homme* (2005): 175–6.

———, and N. Heinich, "La fiction, dehors, dedans," *L'Homme* (2005): 175–6.

Gary, R., *The Roots of Heaven*. New York: Popular Library, 1958.

———, *A European Education*. New York: Simon & Schuster, 1960.

———, *The Ski Bum*. New York: Harper & Row, 1965.

———, *Pseudo*. Paris: Mercure de France, 1976.

———, *The Life Before Us (Madame Rosa)*. New York: Doubleday, 1977.

————, *Europa*. New York: Doubleday, 1978.

————, *Vie et mort d'Emil Ajar*. Paris: Editions Gallimard, 1981.

Gazzaniga, M., *Mind Matters: How Mind and Brain Interact to Create our Conscious Lives*. New York: Houghton Mifflin, 1989.

Hirsi Ali, A., *Infidel: My Life*. London: Simon & Schuster, 2007.

Jacob, S., *Histoires de s'entendre*. Montreal: Boréal, 2008.

Jones, L., *Mister Pip*. Melbourne: Text Publishing, 2006.

Jouvet, M., *The Paradox of Sleep: The Story of Dreaming*. Trans. L. Garey. Cambridge, MA: MIT Press, 1999.

Kennedy, D., *In God's Country: Travels in Bible Belt, USA*. London: Abacus, 2004.

Kis, D., *A Tomb for Boris Davidovitch*. New York: Penguin Books, 1980.

Kozakaï, T., *L'Etranger et l'identité: essai sur l'intégration culturelle*. Paris: Petite bibliothèque Payot, 2007.

Minsky, M., *The Society of Mind*. New York: Simon & Schuster, 1985–7.

Naccache, L., *Le nouvel inconscient: Freud, Christophe Colomb des Neurosciences*. Paris: Editions Odile Jacob, 2007.

Nyssen, H., "Mais à quoi donc sert la littérature?" Oral communication, University of Liège, (Belgium), 17 September 2007.

Pachet, P., *Devant ma mère*. Paris: Editions Gallimard, 2007.

Rouaud, J., *L'imitation du bonheur*. Paris: Editions Gallimard, 2006.

Salmon, C., *Storytelling*. Paris: Editions La Découverte, 2007.

Shakespeare, W., *Romeo and Juliet*.

Todorov, T., *On Human Diversity: Nationalism, Racism and Exoticism in French Thought*. Cambridge, MA: Harvard University Press, 1998.

———, *Hope and Memory: Lessons from the Twentieth Century*. Princeton, NJ: Princeton University Press, 2003.

de Waal, F., *Our Inner Ape*. London: Penguin Books, 2005.

Winnicott, D.W., *Playing and Reality*. London: Routledge, 2005.

ACKNOWLEDGMENTS

My work on this book was also nourished by conversations with Yann Apperry, Chloé Baker, Catherine David, François Flahault, Hervé Matras, Mihai Mangiulea, Karine and Lionel Naccache, Michel Rostain, Katia Salomon and, *last but not least*, Tzvetan Todorov. My heartfelt thanks to all of them.

language
45,147